Creating a Great Home Piece by Piece

GOODHOUSEPARTS

Dennis Wedlick

Photography by Erik Kvalsvik

The Taunton Press

The Taunton Press, Inc., 63 South Main Street, PO Box 5506, Newtown, CT 06470-5506
e-mail: tp@taunton.com

Distributed by Publishers Group West

EDITORS: Marilyn Zelinsky Syarto, Peter Chapman
JACKET DESIGN: Dania Davey
INTERIOR DESIGN: Lori Wendin
LAYOUT: Lori Wendin, Susan Fazekas
ILLUSTRATOR: Sue Mattero
PHOTOGRAPHER (except where noted): Erik Kvalsvik

LIBRARY OF CONGRESS CATALOGING-IN-PUBLICATION DATA:
Wedlick, Dennis.
  Good house parts : creating a great home piece by piece / Dennis
Wedlick ; photographer, Erik Kvalsvik.
     p. cm.
Includes index.
  ISBN 1-56158-628-5
  1. Building--Details. 2. Woodwork. I. Title.
  TH2025 .W42 2003
  728'.37--dc21
                          2003012784

Printed in the United States
10 9 8 7 6 5 4 3 2 1

To my mother,
whose good advice inspires
me every day

Acknowledgments

GOOD HOUSE PARTS would not be possible without the work of good architects. This book features the work of five architectural firms: Bohlin Cywinski Jackson; Charles Warren, Architect; Michael G. Imber, Architect; Centerbrook Architects; and my own firm, Dennis Wedlick Architect.

Peter Bohlin, of Bohlin Cywinski Jackson, is the designer of the waterside home in Rhode Island that is featured at the end of the section on "Quality." I can think of no other architectural firm in the country that can exceed their standard of quality, which is expressed through careful attention to the smallest of details. Upon close inspection, even a simple handrail on a Peter Bohlin house will be revealed as a work of art, a celebration of the full potential of humble building materials.

Charles Warren's design for a family in New Hampshire is one of the finest homes I have ever visited. Charles is a master of proportions, and every detail of one of his homes is close to perfection. His homes are some of the most lavishly detailed and seemingly most expensive homes in this book—not because they are the grandest or were the most costly to build, but because they are so rich with character and good architecture.

Michael Imber's projects are featured throughout this book, and their parts have a quality that is comparable to fine jewelry—something to be considered when a little extra money might be spent here and there. Any tour of the homes of the rich and famous would quickly prove that using the most expensive materials doesn't necessarily guarantee a good home. It takes a very talented architect, like Michael, to be able to use high-end materials in a way that is worthy of their value.

Homes designed by Centerbrook Architects are featured in many books on residential architecture and for good reason. They have a playful, almost stylized knack with house parts that gives their homes the strong character and sense of place that so endears their work to the owners. The house shown on the front cover of this book was designed by Centerbrook and features a rich miscellany of parts: good windows and doors, good trim, good materials, and good details, to name just a few.

For my own part, I'd like to acknowledge all the people in my architectural firm who have made our clients' dreams come true. I am fortunate to work with the finest architects, who are also caring and supportive.

A good home is the result of a successful collaboration between the homeowners and the people they commission to realize their dream, and I'd like to thank all of the homeowners who allowed us into their homes to photograph their Good House Parts. And a special word of thanks to photographer Eric Kvalsvik, whose ability to recognize and capture the elements of good design is unparalleled.

I would also like to acknowledge everyone at The Taunton Press who helped me to create this book. Without Marilyn Zelinsky Syarto, Maria Taylor, Jim Childs, Paula Schlosser, and Peter Chapman, I would not have known where to begin. Thank you all for your continued support and hard work.

Finally, home is really only where the heart is, and my heart is always with my partner-in-life, Curt DeVito. To my parents, his parents, and our large and wonderful family, thank you all for being there.

CONTENTS

Composing with Good House Parts

OUR COUNTRY HAS A HISTORY of building good homes in a wide variety of styles and designs that reflect the diversity of our cultural and ethnic roots. From traditional homes to modern contemporaries, a well-designed home, regardless of the style or era, starts with a thoughtful composition of what I call "good house parts." Good house parts range from the smallest details, such as the pattern of storage cubby holes in a mudroom to the shape and pitch of a cottage-style roof. And each part reflects the creative, collaborative vision of a homeowner and his or her architect and builder. How these parts are conceived, designed, and uniquely combined is at the heart of every well-designed home.

The intriguing notion of thinking about houses as a collection of good house parts is rooted in the idea that a good home does not need to slavishly follow every aspect of a particular architectural style. For instance, it's possible to combine the warmth of a bungalow interior with a whimsically inspired Victorian front porch. An experienced designer can find a way to incorporate elements from both styles into one good home. The important thing is that a new home or renovation is inspired by how it will be lived in, by the family's lifestyle, and by the owner's personal vision.

After designing and building dozens of homes over the last 20 years, I've come to appreciate four qualities that are essential to composing a good home with a thoughtful collection of good house parts. The four qualities are character, comfort, harmony, and quality. A home with CHARACTER reflects the owner's lifestyle while conveying a strong sense of personality and visual appeal. The uniqueness of homes with character is evident from rambling kitchens for sociable cooking to private retreats for music or meditation. Homes with true character also instinctively include house parts that enhance COMFORT, with a welcoming, truly at-home ambiance.

A good new home starts, of course, with a building lot or a plot of undeveloped land. Creating a house that is in true HARMONY with its surrounding landscape involves choreographing a series of good house parts that accentuate the natural setting. For example, the windows may be designed to frame a special view or to capture the cooling breezes on a summer's night. Finally, the thoughtful use of QUALITY materials, whether in the front porch columns or the breakfast nook benches, provides a sense of timelessness, creating a house that is built to last for generations.

The Roots of a Good Home

Our nation's first residential architects made it their mission to create affordable, quality homes for every American. They originated the idea that each individual could have a well-built, unique home. The architects of this picturesque vision were our nation's first residential designers. A. J. Downing, father of the home design book, wrote that all Americans should have homes that reflect their individuality, the beauty of their inherited landscape, and their free society. Yet, for much of the last 50 years, this vision has been an elusive one for many Americans. Traditional approaches to home building and design have not consistently created homes that are imbued with character, comfort, and enduring quality. Many suburban housing developments have lost a sense of neighborhood and true character, leaving homeowners with few choices but to settle for a house that lacks personality and charm.

Increasingly, however, homeowners, architects, and builders are successfully collaborating both to renovate existing homes and to craft a generation of new homes that will become tomorrow's classics. This new level of creative energy is a promising start to a movement that will grace our communities and neighborhoods with houses that have been carefully

A built-in blackboard, wainscoting, and a plate rail are three house parts that make this eat-in kitchen a memorable room.

A home that's in harmony with its setting, such as this small cabin that takes full advantage of its view, always seems larger than one that turns its back on it. The simple trim surrounding the ganged casement windows draws the focus of the room to the serene woodland setting.

One good, well-positioned window with an attractive pattern of panes will make an ordinary view special and a good view outstanding.

composed and informed by a vision of a truly good home.

Starting with a Personal Vision

A good home cannot be designed with one brilliant insight, nor does it follow one simple design recipe. If it is to be successful, it must be created step by step specifically for the homeowners and the physical setting. The design of a new home or a renovation of an existing one needs to be considered piece by

piece, pulling together the individual house parts based on the needs and desires of the owner.

Every home featured in this book was custom tailored according to the personal vision of the owner. These homeowners worked hard to create a dwelling that reflects their lifestyle, personal design aesthetics, and dreams. And these ideals can be applied to any new home, addition, or renovation. Whatever the project, it is possible to create a quality, comfortable space to fit almost any budget that will last for years to come. The diversity of the homes

Every member of the family can benefit from a well-placed bench, whether to take off muddy boots or just to take in a little sun.

featured here reflects the range of desires from expansive porches with wide-open views to social spaces for family fun to intimate rooms for musicians and bookworms. Whether formal or rustic, a good house has true character, is comfortable to live in, is crafted with quality materials, and harmonizes with the surrounding landscape.

Character Starts with a Story

A house has a strong sense of character when it expresses the owners' personal tastes, interests, and dreams. I like to think of these qualities together as the story of the house. Each home's story has central themes, ideas, and an almost visible plot line that informs its design. Most homes' storylines are expressed in a series of design ideas that, when woven together, make a house intriguing, interesting, and the subject of continued conversation and enjoyment for many years.

A good house can be realized through a variety of life experiences. One homeowner may dream of a "house that would be like a rustic pavilion, wide open to the woods that surround it"; another might envision "a house that would appear to be an assem-

The shape of a home's exterior walls and the arrangement of its windows are the essential ingredients that make the most of its interior spaces and its setting. Here, the glass walls overlooking the deck blur the lines between inside and out.

blage of elegant structures, as if built over time." Some people have such a vision already formulated in their minds and seek a location that can be developed to fulfill it. Others come to their story after purchasing a property and seeing how their home can be nestled into the landscape. It is this personal vision or story that separates an ordinary house from one that has enduring, engaging character.

Only a few well-chosen good house parts are needed to convey an interesting story. For a rustic pavilion, these might include the shape of the roof, the particular selection of the exterior and interior trim details, and the use of a few good design techniques that seem to bring the outdoors inside.

Similarly, in an elegant house that appears to be built over time, the vision could be realized through use of a particular detail that expresses a feeling of graciousness. For example, a crown molding in combination with a design technique that sculpts the home into a series of wings or additions gives the sense that the home has been gradually changed over the years.

The best designs accomplish the essence of the story with minimal effort. Too many bells and whistles can detract from the essential beauty and spirit of a home. This is the fundamental reason why homes with real character can be affordable. I built a "castle in the forest" for one couple who had a very tight budget. Their castle was only 800 sq. ft. and was built of wood shingles, not stone. Yet it had all the romantic features and qualities that its owners longed for…a stair tower, a sense of solitude and fortitude, and even a gesture at the front door that calls to mind a drawbridge. The details and materials were not medieval or exotic by any means. All were found at the local supply store. It's just that certain house parts, such as the cedar shingles, the concrete blocks, and even the asphalt siding, had the right texture and color to give this tiny

A unique combination of good house parts, each with its own charm, can add up to a breathtaking room. Here, ornamental arch-topped French doors are set into an otherwise modern design.

Certain combinations of good house parts can achieve seemingly opposite effects. These oversize French doors and double-hung windows combined with a rustic wainscoting create an interior that's both modern and breezy and, at the same time, rural and cozy.

Every detail of a home can contribute to comfort. These steps that lead down to a sunken living room were designed to serve as extra seating, a side table, and a bookshelf.

By themselves, these custom kitchen cabinets are beautifully built. Combined with a perfectly square window set symmetrically between the tall hutches, they create a kitchen full of character.

for winter warmth. And in another setting this means a wall of windows to capture a spectacular vista.

The good home is fitted to accommodate every one of life's ideal scenarios: the perfect place for eating breakfast, entertaining friends, and finding privacy. Even laundry can be a comforting task when a home is designed according to your preferences. Creating a home that adds comfort to your life starts with choosing the appropriate good house parts that match your personal sense of comfort. For each notion of comfort there is a corresponding house part. House parts that create a sense of com-

fort tend fall into three categories: those that help organize the home; those that make the most of the interior spaces; and those that facilitate the movement throughout the house. The best combination of these good house parts results in a recipe for a house that feels like home the minute you cross the threshold.

A Home in Harmony with the Land

The best homes make the most of their setting and the natural landscape. A home's setting embraces not only the immediate surroundings but also the distant views. It includes all the natural features of the land from the nearest big tree to the way the sun rises over the back of the house. Yet for many people the setting begins and ends at the front and back yard. Taking a more expansive view of how the land and the house work in harmony results in a home that has a natural sense of place with intriguing views, an experience of the sun's daily path, and a thoughtfully designed site.

Before there is ever a house, there is the raw land. It might be an empty lot in a development, a small plot on a remote beach, or an urban lot in a rejuvenated neighborhood. Starting with the land is the first test of a personal vision of a good home. It

The gracefulness of this room, conveyed by the airy shelving and bright box window, contrasts nicely with the sturdiness of the stone wall.

brings a vision into clear focus, making an original design idea work within the boundaries and contours of the land. Many times, the property itself will build character into the house with the incorporation of several thoughtful good house parts that play to the best features of the site. Perhaps you've always imagined living in a brick cottage with a steeply pitched roof and deep-set windows. But if you buy land on the coast of New England, the cottage would be better clad in the cedar shingles that are found typically in those parts.

Windows, a house's eyes to the outside world, should be arranged to take advantage of the property's views whether they are of a mountainside or a single oak tree. A home in harmony with its site opens up to the sunshine and breezes while enjoying overarching shade and protection from the harsher forms of these same elements. Everyone's home should have good house parts that allow people to make the most of the outdoors, such as open or screened porches, windows that allow a morning breeze to flow into the kitchen, or an outdoor fireplace for late-fall cookouts.

I know first hand that using the right combination of good house parts can deliver not just a better home but a better life. At 25 ft. by 15 ft., the first floor of my own house in upstate New York is smaller than many of my clients' living rooms, but it is the perfect size for two. But if we have any more than a couple of guests, the space is inadequate. We like to entertain and knew we needed to make a change, but we didn't want it to ruin what we like about the house.

One addition with the right good house parts did the trick. We built what we call our "party barn," with a great cooking area, plenty of storage, a living space crafted of rough-and-tumble materials, and room for a sit-down dinner for any number from four to forty. The building is uninsulated, has big screened openings that can be closed off from the rain with solid barn doors, and is not attached to the house—which means it is good only for warm-weather parties. For the same cost, we could have doubled the size of our tiny house, but we would never have been able to accommodate a crowd. It is the uniqueness of the barn, the special recipe of its parts, that has transformed where we live to better suit our lives.

An angled built-in at the edge of a sleeping loft is a useful and decorative addition.

Quality in the Details

There is a general misconception that good homes are no longer being built because quality materials and fine craftsmanship are extremely expensive. That is simply not true. Good house parts are available to fit almost any budget. With careful planning and a bit of research, a quality design can be married to stock parts to create a house that is solid, comfortable, and appealing. Not all good house parts need to be custom built. For example, attractive doors can be handcrafted or can be chosen from a less-costly line from a national manufacturer. A search through the local lumberyard or salvage warehouse and even the Internet is likely to uncover the perfect—and affordable—window, door, column, or hardware to enhance the character and personal vision of a home.

Every good architectural detail in a custom-built high-end home has an affordable counterpart that is readily available.

Exploring Good House Parts

If you look at two homes that are of the exact same size, the one built without quality materials and construction methods will be less expensive than the one designed with a selection of good house parts. But a home built without the necessities of plumbing, heat, electricity, insulation, and weatherproofing would also be less expensive. In my opinion, good house parts are just as essential in making a house an interesting and joyful place to live.

A home that includes only a few good details will be substantially better than one that has none. A home that has fine proportions, takes in the views, and is visually expressive costs no more to build than one crafted from the same materials but without these good house parts. The simple solution for mak-ing it all affordable is thoughtful, advanced planning: distinguishing the good house parts from the bad and discovering the parts that will add up to the ideal home to suit the owners' individual needs, lifestyle, and desires.

Regardless of its layout, size, or style, every house can be a good home if the design or renovation selects from a palette of tried-and-true details and combines them in a way that is best suited to the homeowner and the property. *Good House Parts* is a tour of great materials, successful details, and proven design principles, designed to encourage and empower everyone to achieve his or her own personal dream home by revealing that it's all in the parts.

The author's house and barn are about the same size, but they each have their own distinctive personality.

CHARACTER

CHARACTER

A HOME WITH CHARACTER is emotionally satisfying to live in because it allows you to express yourself. There's no one formula for bringing character into a home, but there are a few basic ways to begin, whether you are designing a new home, adding on, or renovating an existing house. The house's shape, trim details, window and door shapes and sizes, and

roof profile—all good house parts—offer opportunities to lend a home expression and character. These features are like the lines on a face that give a person character.

The shape of a roof immediately signals a home's character. A steep roof on a small home calls to mind a storybook cottage, whereas a low-pitched roof with broad overhangs appears strikingly modern.

An addition to a home—a rather large part—is an opportunity to transform an ordinary house into a distinctive house by reinventing its profile. Smaller parts, like trim details such as brackets, rafter tails, and porch posts, can infuse a home with character. The style of a home can often be defined just by the way the windows are trimmed.

There's a whole world of picturesque house parts that are often neglected in new home construction. Dormers, stair towers, and turrets may sound like details only for whimsical or historic houses, but they can each add a large dose of character to any home. Even something as seemingly minor as an unusual chimneytop can have a significant impact.

Character comes in any size budget and can be store bought or custom designed. A home can develop its character over time, piece by piece, and doesn't have to follow a single stylistic theme. All that's required is a careful choice of parts to reflect the distinctive personality of your home.

The owners of this Florida beach house were thinking outside the box when they decided to add a circular screened porch to bring character to an otherwise square structure.

CHAPTER 1

Discovering the Shapes

EVERY HOUSE HAS A SHAPE, WHETHER IT'S the familiar shape of a simple saltbox or an unusual shape, such as an octagon house. A house's shape is the foundation for its character, so an upright two-story Federal-style farm with a tall dormered roof will have a quite different feel than a ground-hugging, one-story ranch with a broad overhanging roof.

A house's shape is established by three things: the layout of the rooms and the corresponding exterior walls; the number of stories and the shape of the house's roof; and the number and arrangement of any wings and additions. Taken together, they give a home its individual silhouette.

A wide variety of shapes can be combined in one house as long as the proportions and profiles are balanced and harmonious. For example, a cottage with a steep roof may have an ample addition added to one side with a roof of the same pitch, or smaller additions

The exaggerated roof angles shield this southwestern home from the harsh sun and at the same time create a strong roof profile that reflects the dramatic character of the surrounding landscape.

The rambling and overlapping roof shapes of this newly built New England home reflect the way that older farmhouses in this rural area were built addition by addition over time.

with flat roofs can be made on two sides for a strong visual contrast. The more unusual the shapes incorporated into a design of a new home, the less monolithic the results will be. A big, tract home with a bland exterior and little character can be completely transformed by a renovation that adds a ziggurat wall and a large overhang to a new great room, creating a delightful interruption in a sea of mediocrity.

Shapely Walls

The overall shape of a house is determined by the layout of its rooms. For example, a center-hall colonial with rooms on two floors in a four-square layout necessarily results in a shoebox shape with a pitched roof on top. There are endless possibilities for laying out rooms, and the best designs take advantage of the potential of the site in terms of sun, views, and landscape.

When a home is not restricted to a boxlike shape, its layout is free to flow, turn corners, and jut out as needed for the best results. Incorporating shaped walls into the design will give a house a strong character that is expressive of its setting and its occupants. With added angles and curves, an exterior wall can reflect a particular landscape, such as a curving wall that follows the crest of a hill. A pair of small angled walls reaching out toward a beachfront can focus a house toward a panoramic view of the ocean and call to mind the prow of a ship.

Large sections of homes that are made of strong undulating profiles make bold statements and provide dramatic interiors. An unusual contour on the exterior of a home can be the decorative touch that sets it apart from the rest of the neighborhood.

In this Texas house built from a collection of shapes, each turn of the wall creates nooks and alcoves for dining, bathing, or just taking in the view.

The shapes of the two steeply pitched gables complement the surrounding jagged contours of the mountaintops. The smaller 2-ft.-deep gable in the foreground breaks up an expanse of wall to give the house a cozier, more rustic look.

FACING PAGE One way to add drama to a conventional flat wall is to create an undulating all-glass wall of windows. The single-pane windows on the ground floor allow an expansive view of the countryside, while the zigzag shape adds a modern flair to this otherwise traditional barn-shape family-room wing.

LEFT Unusually shaped walls and a faceted lookout tower lend a fanciful air to this modest beachfront retreat.

RIGHT New walls, dormers, bay windows, and a massive chimney change the shape and character of this renovated cottage.

Roof Profiles and Overhangs

More than any other part, the roof is responsible for the shape of a house. Roof shapes should be practical and appropriate to the region and climate (steep roofs shed snow, while low overhanging ones block the hot sun), but there's plenty of room for variations.

Each roof shape gives a different look to a home. A steep roof emphasizes the vertical and encourages you to look up, in much the same way that a skyscraper or cathedral draws your gaze skyward. A low-pitched roof can be equally dramatic because it exaggerates the horizontal dimensions of a house, especially when the roof has a broad overhang. A hip roof, which meets the walls of the house on all four sides, recedes from view, while a gable roof, which meets the walls on only two sides and has a triangular end on the other two sides, calls for attention. Complex-shaped roofs that combine gables with hips or varying angles (such as gambrel roofs) offer opportunities to create eye-catching shapes.

Roof overhangs create additional options for shaping a house. Roofs with only a narrow overhang tend to make a house look like a solid block, tight and proper, whereas deep overhangs are like sheltering canopies providing a more comfortable, relaxed appearance. A large overhang has a great visual impact because it cantilevers out from the wall, forming a striking profile and casting a dramatic shadow on the house below. The strong shape of the roof overhang combined with the play of the shadows it casts against the walls gives even a modest home an alluring appearance.

The steep angle of the roof gives this Colorado house a shape reminiscent of a Swiss chalet— a fitting image that blends in with its alpine setting. The deep, 5-ft.-wide overhang shades the interior from the sun.

LEFT A small house appears larger when it has a roof with a shallow pitch. The flat-pitched roof and shallow overhang allow more of the wall to show.

LEFT A shallow overhang gives this house a balanced, modest appearance.

RIGHT A roof that's flush with the exterior wall can make a house look more formal. Here, the lack of overhang puts greater emphasis on the brick wall.

An oversize, steep roof that comes close to the ground gives this relatively large house a cottage-like character.

The conventional pitch of this unconventional home gives it a more modest appearance than its size would suggest.

ROOF PITCH

Different pitches evoke different visual reactions.

Shallow pitch—eyes look across

Standard pitch—eyes rest

Steep pitch—eyes look up

CHAPTER 2

The Style of the Openings

WINDOWS MAKE A HOME LIVABLE, letting in light, air, and views. The size, type, and patterns of the windows give a home a sense of character and allow it to fit in with the site. The spacing of the windows, the number of glass panes within each window, and the size of the windows all create a distinctive pattern of openings in the façade of the home. The more organized and well thought out the pattern, the more expressive the house.

For example, windows spaced an equal distance apart and aligned along their edges—as in a colonial style—give a home a very formal, buttoned-up look. On the other hand, a playful (yet balanced) composition of windows in a variety of shapes and sizes conveys a casual or a romantic character. Large expanses of glass express a modern sensibility.

Window Sizes and Types

Standard windows are available in a wide variety of shapes and sizes, and custom-built windows can meet almost any specification. The particular windows used in any application should reflect the overall style and character of the house.

The standard, traditional windows in older colonial homes were generally sized to be two to three times as tall as wide. Those proportions are an essential part of their design. Creating a home or adding onto a home with a look that is more traditional can mean simply following these rules of proportions for any size window. By contrast, the style of many mid-century modern homes is established by windows that are much wider than they are tall, referred to as ribbon windows. Integrating an addition with the original home can often be accomplished simply by replicating the existing window style.

Even though this window is small, it calls attention to itself because it is a different color from the meticulously detailed and crafted wood siding that surrounds it.

Traditional (and affordable) double-hung windows are used in a modern, unconventional way to wrap the corners of each room in glass, offering a contemporary flair on the interior and exterior.

These modern casement windows are given the proportions of an old double-hung window in keeping with the nineteenth-century character of the other house parts.

PIECE BY PIECE | Keep It Consistent

When adding new windows or replacing existing windows, the key is to keep proportions consistent. The safest bet is to match windows whenever possible and to arrange them in "gangs" if you're looking to expand a view or capture more light. Mixing horizontal and vertical windows on the same façade can be difficult and requires close attention to detail.

Certain types of windows are also associated with particular periods or climates. Casement and awning windows—which swing open like a door or a flap—are a feature of older stone and adobe homes, although they are also found on 1950s ranch houses. Jalousie windows, made of glass slats to catch cooling breezes, are common in the southern states.

Double-hung windows with shutters are reminiscent of the colonial period and New England saltbox houses. Although older double-hung windows had multiple panes, newer houses often have a single pane in each sash. In the cold northern states, the windows were only about 2 ft. wide by 4 ft. high, but in the south, the grand plantation houses often had windows that reached almost from floor to ceiling.

LEFT Multiple panes on ganged windows can be used to underscore the character of a house. The six-over-one pattern that divides the tall double-hung windows gives this house its cottage-like character.

RIGHT Smaller windows would be lost along the length of this dormer, but the grouping of multipaned casement windows creates a well-proportioned, traditional composition.

The patterns of the panes help to blend two different types of windows on this house. The vertical double-hung dormer windows are roughly the same proportion as the horizontal three-pane awning windows below.

The divisions of glass give these two arched windows their distinctive style.

LEFT The small panes of glass on this window create a traditional, old English appearance.

RIGHT Larger expanses of clear glass and a minimal, but asymmetrical pattern of panes on this window makes the composition seem more contemporary in style.

Window Shapes and Arrangements

The way windows are arranged influences the character of a home even more than the type of windows used. We're most familiar with the balanced arrangement of traditional double-hung windows on the façade of a colonial home, but these same windows can produce a contemporary look, if they're grouped together to make a wall of windows or are set close to a corner. Similarly, a row of modern casement windows can be evenly spaced along a wall to convey a more traditional character.

A large picture window can frame a view and provide a focal point for a room. Picture windows work best when integrated with the character of the house. For example, when flanked by two identical double-hung windows, a large window can take on a more traditional feel. A single large window or

---

PARTS IN DETAIL ## Window Pane Patterns

The way glass is divided within a window creates another layer of character for a home. Historically, a window was made up of smaller pieces of glass, or panes, which were framed together with muntins. Today, some standard windows come with a removable wooden grid to imitate a traditional multipaned sash. These grids can be used to change the style of a window or to integrate a variety of windows into a single expression.

Large double-hung windows with a grid of just two panes over two panes look more contemporary than the traditional six-over-six panes. A pattern of muntins can transform a horizontal awning window into a composition of vertical panes that are sized to match the taller double-hung windows found on the

rest of the house. Windows with striking asymmetrical patterns of panes give a house an Arts and Crafts look. Picture windows can be made less stark by the addition of muntins, which create smaller panes that are more in keeping with the proportions of the other windows on the house.

A bold, modern arrangement is to create a wall of large single-paned windows in a variety of shapes to encompass a breathtaking view. These sometimes stark compositions can be mellowed with the careful use of muntins to produce smaller traditional windows, without sacrificing the view. Just a few smaller panes in the corners, proportioned to match the other windows in the house, can work wonders.

Views can be captured in a more traditional house by closely setting multipaned oversize double-hung or casement windows to create a window wall. To make these tall windows more manageable, they can be shortened and capped with transom windows.

MATCHING PATTERNS ON AWNING AND DOUBLE-HUNG WINDOWS

Panes on the awning windows (top row) are proportioned to match those on the double-hung windows (bottom).

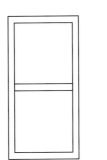

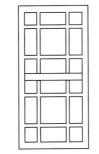

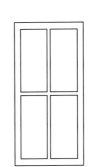

The asymmetrical pattern of panes softens the impact of this oversize picture window. The large opening allows an uninterrupted view of the outdoors, while the smaller divisions of glass give the window a more intimate scale.

LEFT A square bay window on a modest older home looks contemporary with its narrow trim and oversize panes.

RIGHT The bay window on this seaside cottage fits nicely into the pattern of second-floor balconies that offer views of the ocean.

one set into a group of other picture windows is unmistakable contemporary.

While some architectural styles express their unique look in a single style of window, others are defined by the variety of their window shapes. For example, picturesque shingle-style cottages of the nineteenth century featured storybook windows of many shapes, such as eyebrow windows and bay windows. Although the window placement may appear to be random on these homes, they actually make up well-balanced compositions. With a little careful planning, whimsical windows can be incorporated into a twenty-first-century house. A larger bay window may be balanced by a small round window off to one side. A row of round-top second-story windows may be sized to match the exact width of the windows below.

FACING PAGE The upper six-light portions of glass in the bay window are reminiscent of the Arts and Crafts style.

Bay Windows

We typically think of windows as two-dimensional objects, but they can also be arranged to take advantage of the third dimension. Bay windows are the classic example, opening a house to light and views while giving the exterior walls a distinctive profile. Sets of windows of any size can be arranged to jut out from the exterior walls to capture the character of the house. For a dramatic modern look, window walls can be arranged to meet at a tight angle to mimic the prow of a ship. Walls of windows can also be formed into a half-octagon, as in the nineteenth-century gingerbread style, or three windows can be used in a simple, shallow square bay for a contemporary look. These three-dimensional window arrangements can be shaped and detailed to fit almost any style of house and to take advantage of almost any landscape.

This new kitchen bay maintains the traditional look of the existing home. The large windows are proportioned and trimmed to match the the older parts of the home.

LEFT A bay window consisting of three jumbo-size windows and equally hefty surrounding trim brightens up the exterior and interior of a small cottage-style home.

RIGHT Although very different in proportion to the other windows on this home, the picture units of the bay use the same size window panes for a consistent pattern of glass throughout.

Lattice beams, supported by round,
classically tapered columns, create a
casual garden environment that complements, but does not mimic, the
home's other classical detailing.

CHAPTER 3	Selecting the Details

THE GOOD HOUSE PARTS USED TO TRIM THE
walls, roof, windows, and doors and to support
additions like porches and balconies are some of
the essential elements that establish the character
of a home.

Every home is defined by its exterior details.
Two houses of the same size, materials, and shape
will look quite unlike each other if the owners
select different details. Imagine two simple-shaped,
one-story, wood-sided houses. One house has windows and doors trimmed with wide, rustic boards
and a front porch with heavy timber posts. The
other house has windows and doors encased with
colonial-style trim and a porch with classical-style
columns. While one house gives the impression of a
cabin in the woods, the other calls to mind the
homes found along the shore on Cape Cod. Details
alone can make one home very different from
another.

Any exterior edge where two surfaces come
together—whether it's wall and wall, wall and roof,
or wall and opening—offers an opportunity to use
details to accentuate the personality of a home.
Though details are added for practical reasons—
to provide structure, seal gaps, and at times mask
unevenness in the carpentry—trim, posts, and
beams also determine the style of the house. Arts
and Crafts bungalows are trimmed one way, with
neatly cut, wide boards on all sides of their windows, whereas a southwestern-style ranch might
have stucco surrounding the windows with only a
rough-sawn board at the top. Modernist homes are
distinguished by their minimal number of details,
while Victorians derive their character from the
multiple layers of ornamental detail.

Two square columns with classical capitals and bases frame
a simple, oversize window to give the façade of this seaside
cottage an elegant, but unpretentious look. The roof was
extended just 6 in. to provide adequate room for this
added layer of detail and character.

The whimsical detailing of the sill, combined with the blue of the window sash, gives this Florida house a playful air.

The only window trim on this Texas prairie house is a razor-thin strip of wood head trim, which is wider than the opening to anchor the small window to the vast, thick white wall.

Window Trim

Narrow or wide, plain or ornate, window trim is a fundamental house part for determining the character of a house. Modern windows can be tightly finished to keep out the elements with minimal trim, but trim provides an aesthetic transition between the exterior wall and the window opening. Trim can call attention to windows, making them focal points, or it can be used to blend the windows into the overall appearance of the house. The window trim itself can be a bold part of a house that determines the look or style, or it can be subtle, allowing other parts of the house to define its character.

The dimensions, profiles, and color of the material that frames windows and doors determine how the

PIECE BY PIECE | The Defining Line

From a distance, a home's details seem to disappear. For example, standard 3½-in.-wide window trim looks like a thin line in the context of the entire house, but even though it's barely noticeable, it has a significant impact on the look of the house.

trim affects the character of a house. Trim with rough profiles or large dimensions makes a bold, dramatic statement, appropriate for a rugged or whimsical house. Thinner, more delicate trim expresses a refined look, fitting for a Georgian or Victorian-style home.

Since the trim at the top (or "head") of a window is one of the first features on a house to get noticed, a little added trim detail at this point (such as an extra piece of molding or cap) can be an inexpensive way to bring personality to a house. The base of the window frame can add character, too, depending on how far it extends past the frame. To create a Craftsman look, both the head trim and bottom (base) trim are extended well past the side trim of the window.

Wide window trim painted in two shades of bright blue connects four ordinary casement windows and gives this side of the house a playful appearance.

Standard 3½-in.-wide painted window trim and corner boards do not distract from the prominent patterns of the other detailing and materials on this beach house.

Narrow, 1¾-in.-wide window trim gives this house its lighter, contemporary touch. The narrow trim, a modern detail in itself, also emphasizes the expansiveness of the oversize contemporary windows.

Trimming this oversize contemporary window with conventional details of equally oversize proportions at the head and sill gives the house a more traditional character.

ONE WINDOW, THREE TRIM OPTIONS

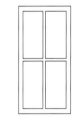

Double-hung window with trim for crisp, modern look

Double-hung window with trim for decorative, layered look

Though this beach house is small, the bright white trim on the arched door is wide and chunky to make this entryway seem larger than it really is.

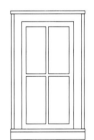

Double-hung window with trim for a rustic look

The roof meets the wall with a razor-thin, 1-in.-wide trim detail. The simple, severe trim creates a clean, contemporary, sculptural look, whereas a wider piece of trim would make the house appear more rustic.

With painted brick-red trim under the eaves and barn hardware for the sliding doors, this house has a distinctly rural character.

PIECE BY PIECE | Detail Consistency

Even plain, flat trim can give a house a look of character when it's used in a consistent way. Treat all sides of your home to the same trim details: Use window casing, edge details, porch posts, and brackets that convey a consistent expression of style. Whether it's a refined classic look or a rugged camp style is up to you.

Exposed painted wood rafter tails underneath the overhang of the galvanized metal roof give this elaborate stone house a more casual, welcoming character.

Trimming the Roof's Edge

Trim at the roof's edges and at the point where the underside of the roof meets the walls greatly affects a house's appearance. To keep building costs down, these areas are often left with little or no trim. Yet adding details at these noticeable intersections goes a long way toward creating a home's character. An elaborate cove or crown molding applied to the edge of a roof can give a house a classic formality. At the other extreme, a razor-thin roof edge complements homes that have few details, such as stucco or minimalist-style homes.

Gutters are often seen as a design constraint rather than an opportunity to make a house stand out from the crowd. There are two main options: decorative gutters and concealed gutters, which are built into the roof edge. All too often a cheap, unattractive gutter (typically of vinyl or aluminum) is tacked onto a home at the last minute, detracting from the expressive possibilities of the roof edge. Exposed gutters can either complement or match the trim on the rest of the house or can make a striking statement of their own. For the best results, the roof edge detail, the gutters, and the gutter material should be thought of as a single well-built house part.

When exposed to the elements, a copper drainpipe and gutter take on the patina of age, adding casual, rural character to this roof edge.

LEFT For a finished, formal appearance, a standard gutter can be clad in wood to look like a pilaster.

RIGHT Rainwater draining through this elongated drainpipe creates the look and sounds of a small waterfall.

The exposed roof beams and supporting brackets immediately identify this house as a ski chalet.

41

Dappled sunlight streaming through the arbor's slats replicates the experience of sitting under a canopy of trees.

Curved rafter tails create a lively design element above a bank of windows overlooking the rolling countryside that surrounds this home.

The open and airy wood trellis contrasts with the patio's heavy stone piers and walls, which match the theme of the other details of this Texas ranch.

Solid cedar posts with equally substantial brackets give this stone lodge home in the Colorado mountains its appropriate rustic character.

Columns and Posts

Porch posts are an often-overlooked design element. The spacing, material, and design of this house part can make a strong statement about the character of the house. Though a porch may need posts only every 10 ft. to support a lightweight roof, posts installed every 5 ft. can create a pleasing rhythm and give the interior of the porch a less exposed feeling. A home with a 12-ft.-wide porch that consists of two fat square piers holding up each end will look completely different from a porch with four equally spaced slender round posts.

The shape and material of the posts, almost unlimited in variety, help determine the style of the house. For example, tapered square wood columns on stone piers at the front entry porch identify the house as a bungalow, whereas Doric columns instantly say colonial. One of the most unusual experiences I've had as an architect involved selecting whole trees to be used as rustic porch posts. The posts alone provided the homeowners with the character they desired for their rural getaway.

To add punch to simple off-the-shelf wooden porch posts, I like to use posts that are a little wider in diameter than necessary—10 in. instead of the usual 6 in.—and place them directly under the porch soffit. The extra width and the clean lines create a dramatic effect.

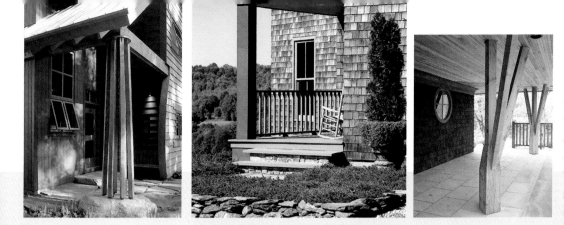

Porch posts display different character.

LEFT A splayed wooden post opposite a curved wall creates a playful entry.

CENTER One robust square column gives a porch a sense of sturdiness reminiscent of an old country farmhouse.

RIGHT Branchlike posts hold up the porch ceiling of this rustic house.

This simple home is dressed up with a narrow porch and columns. The addition of the short, decorative railing above the columns gives the porch a sense of height and makes this composition the focal point of the house's façade.

A cluster of details—such as posts, brackets, latticework, and exposed rafter tails—on a small garden structure brings a storybook quality to the entire yard.

ABOVE **Decorative brackets added underneath a series of deep overlooks add a romantic, Victorian character to this southern house.**

LEFT **The row of thin decorative brackets, running from roof to window trim, on this Texas house recalls the shed-like structures of the early farms of the region.**

Beams and Brackets

Beams and brackets transform roof overhangs and porches into sculptural features, masking their more utilitarian job of supporting overhead structures. Roofs with deep overhangs for shade can give a home a distinct regional character, depending on the design of the posts, exposed beams, and decorative brackets. For example, the wood beams of a home in the Rocky Mountains might be robust and extra heavy to give the exterior a rustic look, whereas the brackets of a seaside cottage might be cut with a delicate filigree to enhance its storybook character. The parts are the same, but the effect is totally different. The nature of a house can be completely changed by these parts. The entry porch of a plain bungalow, for example, can be transformed with the addition of Victorian-style brackets.

A single, chunky, oversize bracket serves as a visual anchor for this front yard entry.

CHAPTER 4 | The Picturesque Parts

ANY HOME CAN BE MADE MORE EXPRESSIVE with the addition of a few picturesque house parts, such as porticos, dormers, towers, and distinctive chimneytops. These parts are prominent yet romantic, and they can be the defining piece to convey a particular character. For example, eccentric trim shapes and elaborate detailing can be used on an entry portico to give a house a Queen Anne or Adirondack camp style look. Applying this level of

detail to the whole house might be impractical, overwhelming—or just plain too expensive—but at a smaller scale, it can strike just the right note and help a house stand out from the crowd.

Adding a tower or turret might seem more appropriate for a mansion or a fortress, but these good house parts can dramatically transform a plain-looking home within a relatively small footprint. Incorporating a steeply pitched roof with dormers can slim down the addition to a not-so-small house, while adding dormers to a remodeled attic can help maintain the charm of a historic home at the same time as it expands the living space. And a clever chimney design alone can set a house apart. It's the way these smaller parts affect the overall shape of the house that gives them the power to have a big impact.

Porticos: Picturesque Gateways

Picturesque house parts have a big effect when used at the entryway, because they are seen close up on a daily basis. Porticos, like porches, provide protection from the rain and snow without enclosing walls. They are used to shelter the entrances of both houses and garages.

Porticos have a lot in common with garden structures such as gazebos and pavilions—all small structures that help set the character not only of the

Stone and wood details give this entryway carport its picturesque quality. The stacked stone walls, treelike posts, and red barn-style roof add charm to a plain house.

An eyebrow dormer is a small but enchanting detail that adds texture, shape, and a quaint character to a house.

This gable dormer sits flush with the exterior wall, breaking up the straight lines of the house.

house but also of the property as a whole. Whether at the end of a brick walk or at the edge of a driveway, a portico that is embraced by a good garden design creates a pleasant and welcoming entrance for guests and family alike.

Dormers of Every Shape

Dormers range in size from small eyebrow dormers that barely peek above the surface of the roof to large, wide shed dormers that are almost minihouses themselves. The specific look of the dormers—how they are trimmed, the way they interrupt the roofline (breaking through the edge or sitting fully on the surface), and their number and spacing—play a big part in determining the character of a house. A series of small, simply detailed dormers allows the

PIECE BY PIECE | Good Dormer Design

The key to good dormer design is not to build too much dormer for the window. The ideal dormer is just a bit larger than the window itself, which should be centered in the dormer. Regardless of the size of the dormer, there should be no more than 11 in. between the window and the outside edge of the dormer.

focus to remain on the main body of the house, whereas a large dormer with an impressive window arrangement and a shapely roof draws attention away from the whole.

Shed dormers have flat sloped roofs, which tend to make them blend in more with the main roof, unlike gable dormers, which have a peaked roof and look like little buildings perched atop the roof. Lantern dormers are so small—with just enough room for a tiny window—that when lit up at night they resemble the lighting fixture they are named for. Low-slung California bungalows have equally low-slung shed dormers, while upright New England center-halls have tall, thin lantern-style dormers.

Without a series of dormers to give a sense of rhythm and composition to this house, the white stucco facade would look stark and austere.

LEFT This tiny dormer brings in light and breaks up the large expanse of the steeply sloped roof.

RIGHT To spice up the façade of this brick house, a dormer with a red copper roof pops up 12 in. above the main roofline.

DORMERS TRICK THE EYE

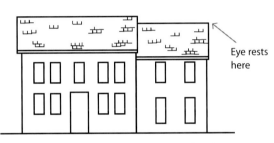

Eye rests here

A two-story addition with a conventional roof looks tall and large.

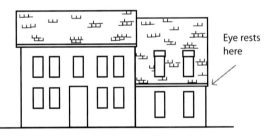

Eye rests here

A two-story addition with dormers looks like a small one-story addition, but it has the same space as the house with the conventional roof.

The design of the dormer drives the architectural character and style of this house. The same wide trim used on the small lantern window (right) and on the three double-height windows highlights the bold lines of the house. A stone chimney adds another layer of texture to this shingle-clad house.

A good way to bring a large second-story addition into balance with the rest of the house is to use dormers. Dormers tend to keep the center of attention off the main roof peak, making the house seem shorter than it really is and reducing the impact of a two-story wall to one story. This keeps the overall scale of the house on a more intimate and cozy level, both inside and out.

Towers Stand Out

Towers and turrets were popular nineteenth-century house parts both on sophisticated houses in the city and on more modest seaside cottages. Today, a tower is defined as a tall structure with a separate

ABOVE An 8-ft.-tall widow's walk gives this small house on a tiny lot additional outdoor space, extra height, and a mark of distinction in the neighborhood.

LEFT A picturesque stone turret makes this house look like a fictional castle. The bay window, placed high on the wall, adds to the tower feeling.

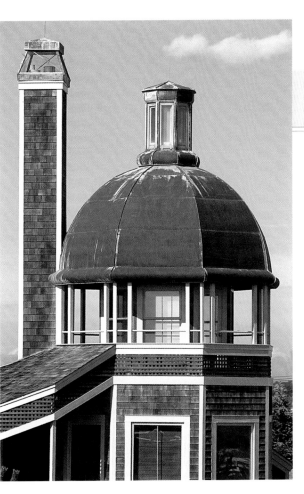

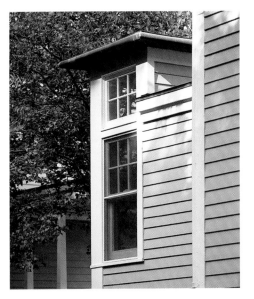

A sense of grandeur is bestowed on this beach house by the exotic domed sleeping porch and dramatic narrow chimney, which rise above the surrounding marshlands.

Incorporating a tower into the design of a modest kitchen addition lets a tiny bit more light into the interior but adds a huge amount of character to the exterior.

roof (a turret is a small tower) that rises above a roofline. Towers are used to accommodate stairways or clerestory windows or to add some variety to the roofscape.

Like dormers, towers jut above the roof and they don't have to be particularly large or elaborate to have a powerful effect on the overall shape of a home. The upper portion of a stairway tower is an ideal place to install windows to bring in light and views. Towers can create memorable spaces, such as an alcove on a second-floor landing or a lookout on a third floor. A stone tower crowned with a classical molding and a copper roof can look grand; with exposed beams and a corrugated tin roof, a tower takes on a rustic character.

Zinc-coated copper is used to clad an otherwise ordinary chimney. The pattern work of the industrial sheet metal adds yet another texture to the various patterns of wood detailing and siding.

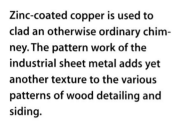

A contemporary look is achieved with this distinctive metal-clad roof part, which houses multiple chimneys and a corner light monitor.

Distinctive Chimneys and Chimneytops

Chimneys and chimneytops are practical necessities for houses with fireplaces; but when playfully designed, they can be as picturesque as towers and turrets. By code, chimneys are required to stand at least 2 ft. above the nearest roof peak, but they can extend higher and be finished off with almost any shape cap. Even prefabricated flue pipes used on modern fireplaces can be clad with built-up chimney enclosures of metal, brick, or wood to add character to a home.

A decorative chimney surround can echo the details found elsewhere on a home. For example, a tapered surround might match tapered columns on

Three chimneys in different materials help shape the personality of each house.

LEFT A rustic stacked-stone pyramid-shaped cap.

CENTER A European-style flat cap on twin stucco chimneys.

RIGHT A colonial-style capless brick chimney.

a porch. The selected size and shape of the chimney will call more or less attention to it. Rounded shapes with small diameters tend to recede and be less commanding than bulky square or rectangular ones. Oversized and unusual shapes will add more to the personality of the house.

Another way to add character to a masonry chimney or chimney surround is with a decorative chimneytop. A distinctive statement here can range from an ornamental pattern fashioned into the last few courses of brick to a one-of-a-kind finish created by a decorative chimney cap.

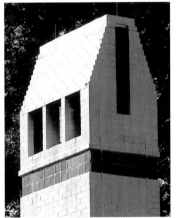

ABOVE The large, chunky brick chimney is perfectly proportioned for this contemporary home built in the style of a farmhouse. Just like all the various large-scale wings and dormers of the contemporary home, each piece gives it the illusion of being a smaller farmhouse.

ABOVE The blue ceramic tiled rim work on the tapered chimney cap adds an eye-catching sculptural touch to the white brick structure.

LEFT These towering chimneys are whimsical expressions of grandeur on this tiny weekend retreat. Their exotic, tapered caps are a highly ornamental detail on an otherwise starkly detailed home.

A Big Texas Welcome

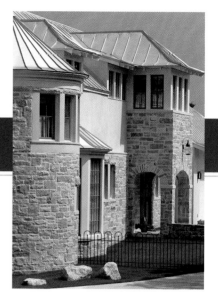

DRIVING THROUGH THE LOW HILL COUNTRY of Texas, you can't help but appreciate why there is so much bravado in this state. Everything in Texas seems as big as Texas pride; even the "low hills" look more substantial than the much higher Catskill Mountains in my hometown in upstate New York.

Erin and Carlos Richter are both Texans, born and raised there and proud of it. They wanted their new house to be all about the best of their state's heritage and history. And they also wanted it to be an expression of Texas hospitality, which is as generous as it is affable. Designed by Michael Imber, the new house is a combination of parts—castle-like towers combined with down-home rocking porches—that capture the unique character of the welcoming Texas heritage.

What makes this house so impressive is that is has character on every side, not just the front. These fanciful turrets run along the narrow side yard of the home's relatively small lot.

A Welcoming Approach

The house is spacious, built from the finest Texan stone, but as guests approach they are not confronted by an imposing front door or an overwhelming statement of the home's true size. Instead, guests are greeted by an intimate and inviting front porch, which helps establish the house's friendly character. It's the sort of porch that might overlook a lake or a spacious backyard, but here it faces the view that embraces the Richters' beloved neighborhood.

The house sits in a suburban development with small lots that have distant views to the Texas hills and surrounding countryside. The inspiration for the home was a nearby historic town that features nineteenth-century "Victoriana" buildings, simple stone structures that are dressed up with a mix of fanciful Italianate and Baroque touches. The Richters' house

The porch's Victorian period details, such as the classically detailed posts and curved steps, express the history of the area and add a layer of character to the entire house.

This rambling country manor–type house is located in a suburban area. The position of the porch allows the family to take in the distant views as well as wave to neighbors passing by.

The large winding stairs set in a stair tower combined with the simplicity of the details—the straight forward railings and posts, the exposed rafter ceiling, and the smooth painted walls—appear playful and comfortable, not pretentious.

The front entryway's exposed beam ceiling and stone flooring mimic the porch's architecture to create the same impression inside and out, a mix of the rustic and elegant.

is a compound of forms built from the same materials and details to convey the same romantic imagery. Small towers, turrets, bay windows, and arcades ring the house, each looking out over the hills and serving as a striking backdrop to their neighbor's yards.

An Informal Entryway

The welcoming porch sets the tone for the house, and the Richters were keen to maintain the "kick off your shoes and stay a while" feeling throughout the interior. Inside the front door, guests are greeted in a large stair hall with a grand staircase and an unusual round landing. But the parts themselves—handrails, newel posts, and square balustrades—are simply detailed to create an air of informality. As on the porch, the entry hall ceiling is lined with exposed rafters, which complement the unassuming front doors.

Using simple versions of Victorian trim, a small but elegant stone fireplace, and country materials like plank floors and beadboard ceiling, the living room is both grand and homey.

The classic composition of these windows expresses the whimsical character of old Texan Victorian houses from the nineteenth century.

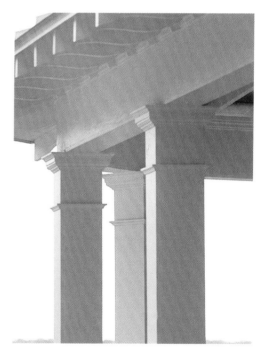

Character is woven through every aspect of this house. Exposed rafter tails meet the refined lines of the decorative porch posts to give the exterior of this house its eclectic quality.

The stone fireplace is tucked to one side of the living room so that it does not overwhelm the space. The emphasis stays on the views out beyond to the hills.

A PLAN CRAFTED WITH CHARACTER

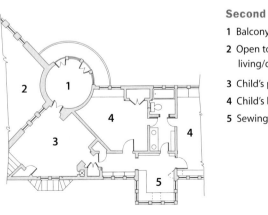

First Floor

1 Bath
2 Master bedroom
3 Terrace
4 Rotunda to master bedroom
5 Two-story living/dining area
6 Fireplace
7 Den
8 Stair turret
9 Victorian entry porch
10 Breakfast turret
11 Kitchen
12 Garage

Second Floor

1 Balcony turret
2 Open to two-story living/dining space
3 Child's playroom
4 Child's bedroom
5 Sewing room tower

Interior Details

The whole interior is generously proportioned and elegantly laid out yet quite simply detailed. Exposed ceiling beams and flat trim around all windows and doors (with just a touch of crown molding) generate an overall feeling that is more Texas country house than French château. When a more elaborate house part is introduced, such as the two-story stone fireplace, it doesn't take center stage but is set off to the side, where it can be discovered as a pleasant surprise.

The wall of windows and French doors frames the view of the Texas hill country. The clerestory windows in the entry hall borrow the light from the upper-level windows in the double-height living room.

The sewing room has ample built-in storage and lots of windows for natural light—all good home parts that promote comfort and harmony in a home.

In another house, the fireplace might have been the focal point, but the Richters wanted the great view of the outdoors to be the main feature of the interior living spaces. From the front door, the Texas hill country is visible through a wall of windows on the back wall of the living room. Standing in front of the expansive view, guests find it hard to believe the house is in the heart of the suburbs.

The living room's beaded-board ceiling is something you might expect on an outside porch, but it

The children have the run of the second floor with a large playroom that looks over the living area and bedrooms that are tucked into the roof with dormers.

serves two purposes here. While this type of ceiling treatment would have been a refinement on the porch, here its texture and character bring a touch of the outdoors to the cathedral ceiling. In addition, the shiny painted wood surface reflects the daylight streaming in from the clerestory windows. A polished, plastered ceiling might have done the same, but the textured surface is informal, in keeping with the intended character of the house.

A Well-Crafted Room

Upstairs, the sewing room is one one of the most comfortable and well-used rooms in the house. It sits at the top of a square turret with windows on three sides that fill the space with natural light. Plentiful built-ins and big work surfaces are paired with beautiful, yet simple, window casings and crown moldings. In this way, the Richters get the best of both worlds, a room that is chock–full of character but at the same time expressly functional.

The windows are trimmed with flat, painted wood boards, carefully composed so that there is no drywall to interrupt the rhythm of the wraparound windows. The narrow molding that caps the extra-wide trim board at the head of the windows provides a neat, crisp edge before the tapered ceiling begins. This tiny room, humble in its function, is regal in its combination of house parts.

to making the various house parts come together in an attractive way are to use balanced composition, good proportions, and compatible finishes.

Two sets of styles are about all that a house can handle. In a balanced composition of two styles, one typically dominates and the other is used as an accent. The principal feel of this house is of a fancy Texas Victorian; the simple Texas country details relax the house's personality.

The entry porch is surrounded by wood columns with nineteenth-century details. Its solid stone floor, set in front of the stone house façade, and

An everyday neighborhood looks distinguished as seen through this picturesque porch with its classical columns, curved shape, and tapered ceiling with exposed beams.

With the right combination of house parts, it's possible to blend two seemingly incongruous styles into a cohesive whole. The Richters' front porch is an excellent example of how pieces from one distinct style, such as the classical details of Newport mansions, can be married to those of a completely different character, such as the bungalows of the Texas hills. The keys

its standing-seam metal roof are elaborate house parts. The ceiling, however, is "country" in its feel, with exposed beams and a planked soffit. Although from a completely different style, the beams are perfectly sized and spaced to complement the more formal parts, and everything is painted a high-gloss white. In this way, plain and fancy work well together to give this house its unique character.

COMFORT

COMFORT

WHEN A HOUSE WORKS WELL for your lifestyle, it's comfortable to live in. Comfort goes beyond furniture. It's all about how you move around and live in the house. A comfortable house should be easy to move through, with uncluttered, well-designed entryways and hallways. A successful home feels roomy because it has a place for everything with

plenty of built-in storage. Theatrical details and special interior amenities in a home bring delightful surprises and pleasures as you go about your day. All these things make a home organized, spacious, and a joy to live in. An interior of uninviting, cramped rooms and hallways can be fixed with just a few good house parts.

A road map for designing a house that works best for you can be drawn by recording the way you move through your house on a daily basis. If your favorite thing to do on a weekday morning is to sit near a window with a cup of coffee, add a built-in window seat for comfort...and storage.

The next step is to evaluate what works and what doesn't. For example, does the laundry room have adequate storage? Is there a quiet place to drink tea and read a book? Is there space near the back door to put down packages? Is there a place for the family computer?

But beyond simple function, a satisfying house is fun to live in and provides spaces that accommodate a variety of moods and activities; for example, a cozy private alcove, a dramatic living room with a cathedral ceiling, and a well-equipped mudroom. A fireplace can play a variety of roles, offering warmth and atmosphere as well as providing a striking focal point. Good house parts, carefully chosen, bring comfort and ease to the routine of everyday life.

CHAPTER 5 The Best Way In, Out, and About

WHEN A HOUSE DOESN'T LOOK OR FEEL comfortable, sometimes it's the way in, out, and around the house that's at the heart of the problem. A house that's easy and enjoyable to move around in never seems too small or too large, whereas a home with poor circulation paths and dead-ends creates wasted and unused space. There are a number of good house parts, such as welcoming entryways, well-equipped foyers, and multifunctional mudrooms and hallways, that can make the interior of a home more efficient and comfortable.

When these transitional spaces are well designed, families will appreciate the reassuring feeling of being able to make the most of every step, from dropping off coats and bags, finding tennis rackets and balls, and picking up the day's mail. The most efficient, comfortable homes are designed to accommodate these everyday activities.

The newly added all-glass back door leading to the garden is visible straight through the house from the front doorway (FACING PAGE), revealing an easy flow in and out of the house.

Entryway and Reception

A good entryway is inviting and comfortable to use. And a good design goes well beyond picking out the front door. It should take into account the approach, the place where you stand in front of the door, what you see when you open the door, and the type of space you're standing in as you cross the threshold. These components play a big part in determining the comfort level of your home.

A series of low, layered decks and wood platform steps make a winding approach to the rear of the house, in contrast to the more straightforward front entry (FACING PAGE).

Exterior and interior entryways work together to create the element of surprise. The homeowners kept this exterior entryway modest (LEFT) but opened it up into a luxurious reception area with a flagstone floor and a mahogany door (RIGHT).

Many homes have a beautiful, expensive front door that is never used because the approach to the door is inconvenient or uninviting. Maybe there's no clear path to the door, or the back door is near the garage and is more accessible and convenient. The approach to the door prepares visitors for the experience they'll have inside the home. If the experience of walking up to the front door is enjoyable, visitors are more likely to feel good about the house when they go inside.

Imagine your entryway as your guests would. Is the entry hidden from view or is it obvious where to go in? Does it look appealing, is it well lit, does it reflect your home's personality? It is not necessary to move the front door to make it more inviting. Adding a sheltering roof over the door can make a big difference. Similarly, enlarging the landing and adding a bench outside the front door can make the entryway more comfortable.

Changing the details can have a big impact, too. For example, replacing the ornate trim on a perfectly symmetrical entryway with plain, flat boards will transform the look from formal to casual.

Inside, the details of the foyer should reflect the rest of the house. The reception area should be sized and arranged so it's large enough for people to linger, yet not too grand that all other rooms in the house feel small by comparison. If the reception is too grand and impressive, it can make visitors feel uneasy—as though they've walked into a public building instead of a private home.

The approachable, human scale of the splayed post, convex wall, and overhead beam creates a dramatic, yet welcoming entrance.

An unadorned, monochromatic glass entryway (LEFT) opens up into a brightly lit space filled with architectural details such as the carved trim above the doors (RIGHT).

Mixing the scale of the elements distinguishes the entry while keeping it comfortable.

LEFT Classical columns form an oversize arch to frame a modest glass door.

RIGHT Once inside, an oversize window dominates the foyer.

The picturesque composition of the front entrance, with its garden gates, stone pillars, window box, curved balcony, and door canopy, warmly welcomes guests.

ABOVE AND RIGHT A spacious mudroom, such as this one measuring 8 ft. by 10 ft., can accommodate the whole family—including the family dog. The glossy painted wood wainscoting and the honed bluestone flooring complement the colors and textures of the rest of the home and are durable and easy to clean. A spiral back stairs allows access to the upstairs, too, a big convenience.

BUILT-INS AT THE BACK DOOR

Even a small space can benefit from multiple built-ins.

1 Storage for umbrellas, gloves, and hats.

2 Key drop with cubbies for bags and backpacks below.

3 Coat hooks.

4 Boot bench with storage.

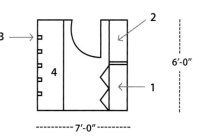

If a house has no reception area, it tends to confuse visitors because they don't know where to stand or look while taking that critical moment to acclimate to the inside of your home. But even if the front door opens directly into the living area, a small reception area can be created by using a different flooring material inside the entry.

The Mudroom

In many homes, the back door is the main everyday entrance to the house—although, ironically, the front door is the one that gets all the money lavished on it. The back entrance and the accompanying reception area (the mudroom) should be just as well designed as the front.

The back door to this large addition to an old farmhouse opens up to a well-organized mudroom with Douglas-fir walls and fieldstone floors. The materials and details were chosen to complement those of the original house.

The mudroom is a transition space between outdoors and in. Although it's one of the most utilitarian rooms in the house, there's no reason it can't be neat and attractive. Built-in benches and cubbies for storage, durable materials such as stone and tile floors, wood wainscoting, and lots of hooks and easy-to-use shelves are key ingredients to a good mudroom.

ABOVE This mudroom was designed as an extension of the kitchen. The storage unit looks like an old hutch with details to match those of the kitchen cabinetry.

The glossy white painted wall surfaces and light-toned hardwood flooring of this brightly lit entryway provide a welcome relief from the surrounding dark woodsy setting on the other side of the glass-paneled doorway.

PIECE BY PIECE | Entry Storage

Entryways can be greatly improved with built-ins and cabinetry. A built-in boot bench with storage below is a better solution for an entrance than a standard coat closet because the entryway can be at least 26 in. wider without a closet. If there's room, add a set of cubby holes in a variety of sizes—small for mail, larger for purses and cases.

The stairway, first-, and second-floor hallways all open to each other, making the core of the home bright and airy.

A renovation incorporated a tiny room off the original stair hall, bringing more light into the interior and creating useful space by adding bookshelves.

Hallways and Circulation Spaces

The inside of a house should be as comfortable and enjoyable to move through as it is to approach and enter. All too often, however, hallways are dark, narrow spaces that do not enliven the interior. In fact, a number of my clients have specifically asked me to eliminate hallways in their new home or reno-vation because these passageways are notoriously uncomfortable and uninspiring. But the answer is not to do away with halls but to transform them into assets that cleverly and efficiently make use of the space.

Ideally, a hallway should be at least 5 ft. wide, which makes it possible to furnish the space or to incorporate built-ins. My house is only 800 sq. ft.,

TYPICAL HALLWAY WITHOUT FOCUS OR STORAGE

HALLWAY WITH FOCUS OR STORAGE

1 Focal point
2 Wide doors for "open" feel
3 Built-in for display and use

Trimmed openings, raised ceilings, and curved walls transform a long hallway into a series of individual spaces, each with its own character.

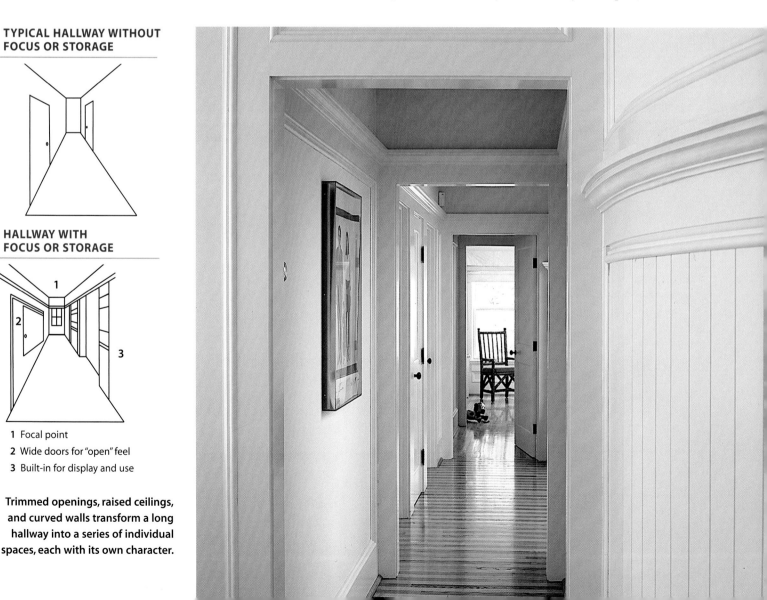

Mixing arched openings with flat-top ones and adding twists, turns, and overlooks brings some welcome pizzazz to an upstairs hallway.

Opening up a hallway to a stairway or living space creates a comfortable, spacious feel.

but I borrowed a few inches from the upstairs bedrooms to create a 5-ft.-wide hallway. The hallway feels surprisingly grand in this small space. In fact, it's just large enough to use as a study.

Windows at one end, or better yet on either side, are essential for making passage through a hallway a pleasurable experience. One way to make an interior hallway less dark is to align the doors of the hallway with the windows in the room beyond. A narrow hallway can be made less claustrophobic if one room off it has a pair of double doors; with both doors open, both the room and the hallway will feel larger.

ABOVE This unusual bedroom door takes advantage of the hallway's high ceilings by adding an operable panel to the top. When both door and panel are open, the room seems to flow continuously from the hallway.

LEFT This narrow hallway with bookcases gets plenty of natural light and ventilation because it is lined with giant tilt-turn windows (which can even be opened when it's raining).

CHAPTER 6	# A Place for Everything

FOR MOST OF US, A GOOD PART OF OUR LIVES is spent preparing meals, doing laundry, paying bills, putting things away, and getting ready for work. Each activity can be more joyful if you have a place for *everything* and you know where to find *anything*. A simple task like folding laundry can be a peaceful experience rather than a mundane chore if the laundry room is well equipped with built-in storage and work surfaces. Every room in the house—from the entryway to the guest bedroom—can benefit from ample, easy-to-access storage. Instead of depending on closet space, adding good built-in house parts will take care of the clutter while enhancing the comfort of the whole house.

Built-ins and cabinets are the best house parts for equipping any room with storage because of their flexibility and resources for efficiency and comfort. As the name implies, these parts are built into the house rather than left freestanding; an example is a storage unit with drawers and shelving that is custom built into a house during a renovation. It's easy to appreciate that built-ins and cabinets can be practical, but they can also be beautiful. The style and detailing can enhance the appearance of the entire interior. There are four essential considerations for a pleasing design: shape, material, composition, and trim.

The smallest corner of a room can be transformed into a useful and comfortable space with built-ins. A corner built-in is in harmony with the other details of this open floor plan, but it is customized to create a fully equipped home office.

A built-in toy cabinet in a hallway leading to a child's bedroom transforms the space into a functional storage zone.

A Shaker-style wall of storage is more spacious than a closet. It neatly holds all of the seasonal and recreational clothing and gear that gets tossed into this mudroom.

Built-in Bookcases and Storage

Kitchens are the epitome of well-planned storage, but with the right built-ins any room can be made just as functional (and as comfortable). We're all familiar with built-in entertainment centers in living rooms and family rooms, but even dining rooms, bedrooms, and hallways work better if they're equipped with adequate storage. Finely crafted built-ins can do the job of freestanding hutches and china cabinets and, as a bonus, transform a dining room into a useful room for other functions. A wall of built-in shelving and cabinets can hold china and linens, and the lower cabinets can be sized and fitted to conceal supplies for a home office or a favorite hobby. The choice of materials and details will determine the look and feel of the room.

Adding built-in bookcases, cabinets, and other storage units does much more for the character and

When the doors of this storage cabinet are closed, they blend seamlessly into the wall. The frameless panels are installed with hidden hinges and precisely match the grain of the Douglas fir of the wall.

A built-in buffet is inserted into a section of this dining room's glass wall to create a privacy screen and storage area.

Built-in bookcases are tools that bring order and purpose to a room. The shallow 18-in.-deep bookcase and storage cabinet makes this hallway space usable.

Dedicating one wall to a built-in bookcase uses the space more efficiently than would freestanding pieces of furniture.

An otherwise ordinary 10-ft.-wide, 2-ft.-deep closet is upgraded with a built-in cabinet that is detailed with trim and wood panels and sized to stop shy of the ceiling. The built-in provides the same amount of storage as a closet, but its delicate, airy design makes the room feel larger.

comfort level of a room than just moving in some new furniture. Built-ins have a look of permanence and can be shaped and sized any number of ways that can distinguish even identical rooms from each other. Children's bedrooms that are similar in size and window arrangements can look completely different with the addition of built-ins. One child's room might have tall bookcases flanking a bed, while another has a run of cabinetry and shelving framing the windows. Secret storage drawers and cozy sitting nooks are other ways to personalize the design of built-ins for each child.

Making a hallway just 18 in. wider than the standard 42 in. allows room to add convenient storage of toys, clothing, linens, or books. Add another 18 in. and the hallway can double as a computer room, a homework space, or even a spillover space for overnight guests.

PIECE BY PIECE | Storage Corners

The key to good storage is not to add more or larger closets in the bedrooms but instead to have flexible, well-organized storage in smaller doses throughout the house. Turn any corner of the house into a storage area by adding built-in chests and cabinets for books, blankets, toys, and even holiday ornaments.

Space and comfort need not be sacrificed when it comes to the laundry room. Ample cabinetry, attractive yet easy-to-clean materials, and a large window to the outdoors can turn this utilitarian space into an inviting corner of the house.

Workrooms and Specialty Storage

For some, a dream home is one with an oak-paneled library or perhaps a sunken hot tub, but for me it's one with a walk-in pantry filled with built-ins. While many homes have a comfortable place for reading and storing books, it's the exceptional home that has the perfect place for storing food, beverages, paper goods, and those really big pans and trays that don't seem to fit anywhere. Other luxuries to consider are a big laundry room, a gardening room, and a workshop.

When space allows, having a room that is set up specifically for a single chore makes sense, especially when that chore is messy. Such areas are best equipped with inexpensive open shelving, a large utilitarian sink, hardy but frugal countertops, and good natural lighting. When space is tight, a small well-designed area off the kitchen may be all that is needed.

Homeowners who specialize in anything from pottery to gift wrapping can easily fill a room with their craft. A space just for wrapping gifts might seem like an outlandish extravagance, but specialty spaces like these, with clever use of built-ins, can make the most of areas that might otherwise have gone unused.

This hobby room is equipped with open cubbies to provide storage for each family member, upper and lower cabinets, and enough counter space for more than one artist.

ABOVE Collections and hobbies can be displayed and stored in hallways, bringing both comfort and personality to a home's interior. This old workbench and the pegged wall that displays a collection of old tools transformed a back hall into a useful and inviting space.

A built-in hamper lets homeowners pass clothing from the dressing room to the laundry room, bringing order to both spaces.

ABOVE **Even the smallest unused corner of a house makes a useful storage area. Cubbyholes transform a 15-in.-wide sliver of a cabinet into a storage center for wrapping paper in this back hallway.**

A well-designed work area, like this kitchen pantry, makes a home more comfortable. It's easy to find the right ingredients in the shallow closet with adjustable shelving, while the nearby prep sink, counter, and cabinetry allow the cook to work efficiently.

This two-sided kitchen island does double duty as a room divider and storage space. The side facing the dining room is detailed to look like a credenza, while the back side blends in with the kitchen cabinetry.

A kitchen island can be a stylistic link to other parts of the house. This custom-built island is trimmed to match the door and window casings and ceiling moldings used throughout the living spaces.

Kitchen Islands

The kitchen island is to today's home what a great fireplace was to a nineteenth-century home: the spot that everyone gathers around. Not everyone cooks, yet everyone uses their kitchen island, one of the most versatile parts of the house. A well-designed kitchen island is well equipped for preparing meals, but also for a range of activities from sorting the mail to grabbing a late-night snack.

An island is more than just another set of cabinets. It can be both a focal point and a space definer, separating one zone for cooking and another for gathering. Unlike other built-ins, an island is visible and usable and is also a stand-alone part. As such, it can be made from different materials than the adjacent cabinetry or room details and can be designed for multiple uses.

The design of the island should take advantage of every surface. For example, one side can match the décor of the kitchen it faces and provide useful storage of cooking utensils, while the other can complement the living spaces it fronts and provide open shelving for books or closed cabinets for entertainment systems. The more carefully the island is designed for all of the adjacent areas, the more flexible it will be.

An extra-tall 4½-ft.-high kitchen island offers double-height storage and conceals the everyday clutter in the kitchen while allowing the cook to converse with family members in the dining and living space.

FAR LEFT The front side of this storage island calls attention to itself because of the sculptural detail that matches the horizontal wood board treatment of the fireplace in the same room.

LEFT The side of this island facing into the kitchen is simple and functional.

Any inconspicuous window seat adds
extra seating without cluttering up
the room with bulky furniture.

CHAPTER 7 | # Making the Most of the Interior

A HOME IS A MORE INTERESTING place to live
when there are special places to enjoy, such as a fireplace to gather around, a window seat for daydream-
ing, and alcoves and niches for quiet retreat. These
house parts increase the coziness and comfort of a
home and can make the difference between a room
that is used and one that sits empty. These are also
the parts that make the most of hard-to-use spaces;
for example, window seats can provide seating
where furniture won't fit, and alcoves and niches can
be tucked under stairs or fit into odd gaps between
rooms or additions.

A stone fireplace with unique wood surround suits
the playful character of this romantic getaway home.

Fireplaces and Their Surrounds

More than any other house part, a fireplace can
bring comfort to a home. Although no longer the
primary source of heat in most homes, fireplaces
still exert a strong emotional appeal—so much so
that even in the desert Southwest, houses with fireplaces are highly sought after.

A good fireplace is more than just the firebox
where the wood or gas burns to throw off heat or a
warm glow. To have a real impact on the room, the
fire, like a view, must be properly framed. The surround consists of the mantlepiece, which is the part

Inexpensive, painted wood planking framing a
12-in.-wide band of slate creates a contemporary
façade for an otherwise plain masonry fireplace.

LEFT A massive stone lintel blends into a field of limestone on this fireplace wall in a southwestern home.

RIGHT The vertical lines of the planking above the limestone hearth add a feeling of height.

A standard-size fireplace is surrounded with a masonry inglenook to give the room a strong focal point. The added built-in bookcases and flip-down desk make the most of this small corner space.

A window seat hugs the curve of this bay window, providing seating for four around the table.

that frames the opening of the firebox, and the outer hearth, which is the part that extends into the room at the bottom of the firebox. Some fireplaces have a hood, which is installed above the mantel and extends up to the ceiling, creating a dramatic effect.

The details and materials of a fireplace surround can add a touch of whimsy, lightness, or natural character to a room that might otherwise be too somber, dark, or formal. A more robust fireplace surround, detailed with a rustic western motif incorporating large stones in its hearth and mantelpiece, might be all that's needed to set the mood for relaxation or fun in a remodeled family room.

The paneled base of this window seat matches the traditional details in the rest of the room.

PIECE BY PIECE | ## Transforming an Unused Room

It sounds counterintuitive, but parts like fireplaces and window seats should be added to the least-used rooms to make the most of a home's interior. Adding a fireplace to a dark, remote, or formal space will automatically transform the room into a romantic gathering spot or a comfortable entertainment area. Adding a window seat to a small, unused library can instantly turn it into a cozy den or reading room.

A large fireplace with an equally large surround can make a room with a cathedral ceiling feel more comfortable because it tempers the grand proportions. The size and shape of the fireplace can be exaggerated by using a wide mantelpiece and a big drum of a hood, both of which can be constructed from drywall and simple wood trim.

Window Seats

After fireplaces, there's no other house part that's as inviting and cozy as a window seat. A window seat that looks out onto a garden or a great view creates a protected, comfortable place from which to enjoy the outdoors. Window seats are natural additions to rooms that have dormers or sloped ceilings, which can otherwise be awkward to furnish because of the low headroom.

Window seats are a particularly efficient house part in that they provide a place to sit while taking

An alcove off a stair hall with a window seat and flanking bookcase serves as a cozy reading nook.

This large alcove off a second-floor hallway is lined with built-in benches with drawer units below. The seating is an extra-deep 36 in., the same width as a twin bed, so it can double as sleeping space for visiting children.

up a minimal amount of floor space. Just 14 in. at the outside edge of a room provides a comfortable roost for reading, knitting, or changing your shoes. Add another 8 in. and there's enough room to take a nap. And the space underneath the window seat makes an excellent chest for storage.

Alcoves and Niches

Alcoves and niches are good house parts that make the most of small, oddly shaped spaces within a home. Smaller than a room yet large enough for furniture, these spaces can be tucked in here and there throughout a home and put to good use. Alcoves and niches can be used to make the most of awkward spaces when planning a new home or renovation or to take care of those odd jigs and jogs

A niche fitted with shelves inside an entry alcove offers a convenient and showy location for a collection of fancy hats.

The built-in booth, placed beside a window, creates a private dining area in an alcove in this kitchen.

The owners of this open-plan house designed an intimate alcove library with a glass-top desk near a window as a quiet retreat. The two niches that flank the alcove are used to display pottery.

A colorful custom bureau converts a niche into a charming built-in storage unit in this seaside home.

that can occur in older homes that have been renovated a few times too many. Left alone, these wasted spaces can look untidy and unattractive, but transformed into alcoves or niches, they introduce another layer of comfort to a home.

An alcove is typically an area off a larger room—it might be the space below a stairway that's fitted out as a children's play corner or a bumpout off a hallway for a computer desk. Niches are usually smaller spaces, shallow in depth. However, if the niche is tall and wide, it can fit a hutch or a dresser; or if small and narrow, it can accommodate a medicine chest.

FINDING SPACE FOR AN ALCOVE

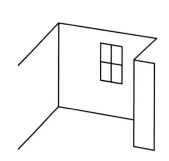

A room with a 14-in. "jog"

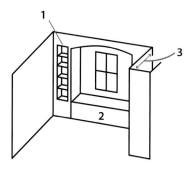

1 Niche for display
2 Alcove for window seat
3 Existing jog

Nothing makes a room cozier for children than a sloping ceiling. These two children's rooms get their small-scale charm from the low kneewalls, the spaces tucked under the eaves, and the dormered windows.

In this serene, glassed-in room, columns frame a focused view of the garden, and the triangular peak lets in additional daylight. The dormer-like ceiling celebrates the view of the garden.

A slightly curved ceiling gives this master bedroom more breathing room and the feel of a four-poster bed.

A flat ceiling would make this small master bedroom feel confining. Following the shape of the slightly peaked roofline adds height and character to the room.

unique and playful, relieving the monotony of the usual flat pancake of space. The availability of flexible drywall makes it possible to add a gentle vault to a hallway at minimal cost.

Cathedral ceilings are most commonly associated with entry halls and living rooms, but they can be just as dramatic when incorporated into a bedroom. If there is attic space above, a bedroom ceiling can be raised, with striking results, especially if high windows are added for additional light or to capture a view. Rooms tucked under the roof with exposed ceilings and dormer windows make for the most cozy and comfortable bedrooms, with walls that seem to enfold you in a comforting embrace.

Stairways

When a home has a no-frills staircase, designed just to get you from one floor to another, it doesn't do a lot to raise your comfort (or excitement) level.

Going up and down a stairway should be an event: admittedly, it's a short journey, but there's no reason it can't be enjoyable. A home that scrimps on stair space almost always ends up with uncomfortable stairs that are steep, narrow, and hard to climb. Good stairs are set at a gentle angle, with wide land-

ABOVE A variety of ceiling shapes and detailing adds interest to this all-white interior. The dining room's vaulted ceiling is a subtle way to define the space, setting it apart from the other rooms in the open plan.

LEFT With an expanse of windows and an exposed wood ceiling, this dining area is both airy and cozy.

This gracious, open stairway is strategically placed to make it a focal point from nearly every room on the first floor.

Stair treads wrap around the railing to create spacious built-in bookcase shelving.

CENTER HALL WITH STAIRS IN MIDDLE

Traditional stair hall blocks light, space, and open feeling.

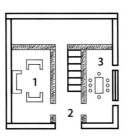

1 Living room
2 Closed hallway
3 Dining room

OPEN PLAN WITH STAIRS ON OUTSIDE WALL

Stairs on the outside wall allow light and views to pass through.

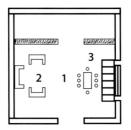

1 Open space
2 Living room
3 Dining room

Three staircases with dramatic designs.

A metal and wood staircase cantilevers off the wall and appears to be floating in the air.

CENTER Windows frame outdoor views on this simple staircase.

RIGHT Stained and painted wood elements in this double-height entryway produce a cozy, rustic character.

ings and turns so that you can comfortably pause as you climb up or down.

Stairways can play a ceremonious role in a house and, if generously sized, can also provide spill-over seating for parties. They are potentially the most theatrical spaces in the home, offering opportunities for grand entries, chance meetings, and passing conversation. When a rarely used room is opened up to a stairway, people going up or down the stair will bring activity to it, and the room will become an integral part of the house.

Stairways can also help adjust the scale of a room. In a large or tall space, an appropriately proportioned stair can make the room feel cozier. In a small home where space is at a premium, the stair can be placed inside a living space rather than in a separate stair hall, which not only maximizes the efficiency of the layout but also adds to the sense of theater. Running a staircase along one wall of a living room or dining room provides a space below for built-ins. When designed as a single unit, the staircase and the cabinetry can become a wonderful focal point.

With so many possibilities for design and detailing, this one good house part plays a major role in establishing the character of the interior. Every individ-

PIECE BY PIECE | A Well-Placed Stair

Run a stairway on an outside wall with windows to take advantage of views and natural light (see the drawing on the facing page). If the stair is open on both sides, with skinny balusters holding up the railing, light from the windows will spill into the room. A stairway on an outside wall rather than in the middle of a room also frees up more interior space.

ual part—the treads and risers, the stringers that support the risers, the balustrades that hold up the railings, and the newel posts that anchor the railings and balustrades at top and bottom—can be fashioned to suit any type of interior imaginable.

One exceptional detail, such as this rounded hand-carved tread end, brings attention to the bottom of the stairway while providing an extra seat.

FACING PAGE This colorful, gently winding staircase has built-in storage to make the most of a small space.

A gently winding set of stairs adds a touch of adventure to every ascent.

CENTER Diagonal steps off a main hall lead up to a master bedroom.

RIGHT A cottage gets its whimsical character from playful cutouts in the stair rail.

ABOVE Natural light brightens up a stairway and upper landing. The hallway at the top of the stairs resembles a bridge overlooking the living room and the backyard, creating a natural gathering place for the family.

RIGHT The mix of spindle and slat railings with decorative holes makes this staircase a welcome feature, rather than an intrusion, in the middle of this room.

A salvaged window divides the dining room from the breakfast corner of a kitchen.

CENTER An interior window opens up a room to the rest of the house. Shutters close for privacy.

RIGHT An interior double-hung window borrows day-light from the double-height family room below.

Overlooks and Interior Windows

While cathedral ceilings can bring drama to modest homes, in large vacant spaces they can have the opposite effect, making a room feel oppressive and uncomfortable, almost like a warehouse space. One way to enliven the expansive space of a double-height room is to add an overlook, which, as the name implies, is simply a second-floor balcony that looks over an interior space. An overlook can provide a focal point for a tall room or enrich the top of a stairway and the spaces adjacent to it.

In a similar way, interior windows can be incorporated high in a double-height space to bring natural light into interior rooms. But they can also be used in a variety of ways to bring light to gloomy corners and dark hallways throughout the house. Adding an interior window to a dark pantry or laundry room located deep within the house makes the room much more comfortable to work in. Interior windows can also be positioned to bring light into adjacent rooms without sacrificing privacy.

ABOVE An interior window opens up a kitchen wall, letting in light and aligning with the overlook beyond to encourage communication between family members.

An indoor balcony off a children's room is a perfect perch for watching what's happening in the living room below.

This interior window acts as a lookout over the double-height entryway.

Tailored for Comfort

COMFORTABLE HOMES, LIKE COMFORTABLE shoes, come in all styles and designs. Bert and Elsie Fichman hired my firm to design a two-story home on the Hudson River in New York State. At our first meeting, they brought with them a huge file filled with images of austere country houses that represented their vision of the ideal home. But with each image they cautioned me that their new home must also be comfortable. It was clear from the clippings the owners were attracted to modern interpretations of farmhouses that had modest exteriors and

a sense of orderliness in their interiors, but the couple was afraid that these designs might not be easy to live with.

With a baby girl and another child on the way, Bert and Elsie wanted lots of child-friendly space with plenty of storage, but they didn't want a house that looked or felt too large. After browsing through magazines and books, they had a sense of what good house parts would fit their needs (and taste): simply detailed living spaces with neat built-ins and handsome fireplaces; and, for the children, delightful bedrooms with shapely ceilings, playful interior windows, and cozy windows seats.

The Benefits of Built-Ins

Bert and Elsie envisioned an interior that would combine the sensibilities of an uncomplicated colonial farmhouse with the conveniences of a better equipped modern home. Few colonists would have enough books or dishes to fill even one built-in, but the Fichmans wanted ample cupboards and bookcases in nearly every room. They realized that

TOP AND LEFT Extra-heavy rustic roof shingles and salvaged Doric-style porch columns add a relaxed rural feel to this house a few miles upriver from New York City.

FACING PAGE Built-in bookcases, cabinets, and window seats make for a gracious, well-organized, and well-used living room. The cabinets hold games, CDs, and a stereo system, and the top of the window seat flips up to provide storage for an army of toys.

Everything in the large main living/dining space is generously sized but well proportioned, so that it feels comfortable but not cavernous. The fireplace, flanked by window seats, is the natural focal point of the room.

A LAYOUT WITH COMFORT BUILT IN

First Floor

1 Garage
2 Kitchen
3 Living/dining room
4 Entry hall
5 Mudroom and potting corner
6 Bike storage
7 Built-in bench and key drop
8 Built-in breakfast bench
9 Built-in window seat and storage
10 Fireplace
11 Children's arts and crafts corner

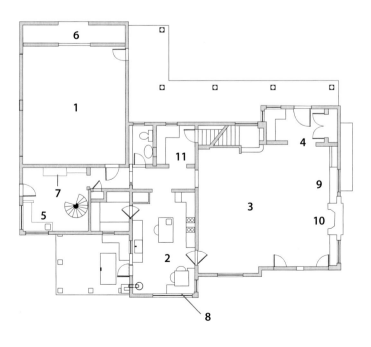

LEFT **A bank of French doors frames outdoor views of a nearby river and the garden, reinforcing the sense of harmony between the house and the landscape.**

RIGHT **A pair of double-hung windows strategically placed next to a broad stair landing brings ample natural light into a potentially dark corner.**

the more places they had to put things, the better chance that things would be put away, which would give them the neat and tidy look they desired. The living/dining room, the bedrooms, and even the baths are all equipped with built-in shelving and cabinetry, and each is carefully tailored for a crisp, clean look.

As in the single-room farmhouses of yesteryear, there are no occasional or formal rooms in this home. The main floor contains one large multi-purpose room that is well appointed with elegant but useful house parts. A federal-style fireplace is tucked between inviting window seats that double as chests for toys. The same wall contains built-in cabinets topped by ample bookcases.

The room is larger and more impressive than the humble rooms of old farmhouses. It has a 10-ft.-high coffered ceiling with a pattern of painted beams, and the walls are punctuated with oversize windows and two pairs of tall French doors. At the same time, these grand house parts make the room feel more comfortable by giving it a good sense of scale: everything feels just the right size—neither too big nor too small.

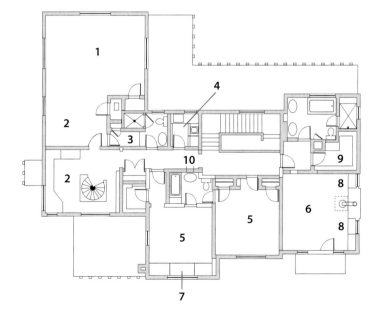

Second Floor

1 Studio/family room
2 Home office
3 Linen room
4 Laundry room
5 Child's bedroom
6 Master bedroom
7 Built-in bench and cubbies
8 Built-in bench and bookcase
9 Built-out closet
10 Interior window

ABOVE Each bedroom has its own unique arrangement of built-ins. Here, a cheery window seat next to open shelves is the perfect place for reading a book or playing with dolls.

ABOVE RIGHT A decorative interior window enlivens both the hallway and one of the bedrooms.

Comfort comes with two bathroom sinks, twice the amount of lighting, and double the built-in storage space.

Purposeful and Pleasurable Parts

All of the elegant details and functional storage parts are made from smooth woods (birch and maple), painted satiny shades of white for a neat appearance. But even though the Fichmans have an affinity for a pure and basic décor, they also wanted a few fanciful house parts that would make their home more relaxed.

Toward the middle of the first floor, a spacious, sunlit stairway with surprisingly decorative newel posts (painted white, of course) runs along the outside wall of the house. At the top of the stairs an extra-wide hallway overlooks the dining area below, featuring interior windows with colorful Victorian glass that open into the children's suite. The kids' bedrooms are tucked into the roof, with sloped ceilings and low kneewalls at one end—perfectly scaled for kids. Small built-ins and low window seats with drawers below complete the children's realm, creating fun, comfortable, yet still orderly bedrooms.

ABOVE Built-in storage tucked in a corner, a wall of French doors that lets in a flood of light, and a small balcony give the illusion that this is a spacious bedroom. The window seat with storage space below fits into the tiniest of nooks. Though no space goes unused, the bedroom feels far from cluttered because built-ins naturally look neat and orderly.

Even the window treatments in this well-conceived home are good house parts. Details like these built-in shutters give the home its unique charm.

The sliding barn door, the planking of the garage doors, and the barn lights are unfussy parts that add a country air to the otherwise refined home.

Personal Exterior Touches

The Fichmans' home appears as comfortable and orderly from the outside as it does from within. The couple wanted the house to have the simple exterior appearance of a country farmhouse but not look out of place in their suburban community. The house is dressed in painted clapboard siding, which is found on homes in the neighborhood as well as on farmhouses farther up the valley.

We added other house parts here and there that acknowledge the family's appreciation for the comfortable simplicity of rural architecture: a wood-planked barn door, barn lights, salvaged porch posts, and a blue-painted front door. But, as on the interior, the few whimsical parts are set into a field of minimalism, simple, painted detailing, and soft unassuming shapes. The garage wing of the home, with its recreation room above, was built in the shape of a barn, which gives the home the look of a traditional L-shaped farm compound.

The wraparound entry porch and the screened porch off the back round out the comfortable, rural feel to this suburban property. The entry porch is wide, connecting the house and garage wings, but not too deep to prevent light from entering the interior. Built from salvaged posts with plain detailing and exposed beams, the porch gives the large house an easy air. The screened porch, shaped like an old lean-to, is built solidly with a stone floor. With a commanding view of the Hudson River, it is one of the most comfortable rooms in the house.

A screened porch tucked into a corner on the back of the house has the comfortable look of an old farm shed.

Defining Parts

For the owners of this house, a well-equipped pantry with beautiful built-ins is the most luxurious of house parts and a worthy investment.

One corner of the mudroom is given over to gardening. Built-in storage and counter space with an angled view of the yard makes this the perfect potting corner.

One of the most impressive things about the Fichmans' house is how much space is dedicated to hardworking rooms. This house is big enough that it could include at least two more bedrooms, a formal dining room, and a library—yet the owners had no desire for any of those spaces. Instead, they have the luxury of using the space for a large mudroom (big enough to include a potting corner), an arts and crafts room, a spacious eat-in kitchen with a walk-in pantry, and two laundry/linen rooms.

Almost as much space is dedicated to everyday chores as is given to entertaining guests; and because there is so much space for doing laundry and potting plants, these mundane tasks are more enjoyable to do. These spaces are filled with natural light, are within earshot of the family gathering spaces, and are well equipped with built-ins and durable surfaces. It's one thing to make a house bigger; it's another to make it more useful. The Fichman's home works because it is beautiful, comfortable, *and* functional.

Every corner of the mudroom serves a purpose: the potting corner, the spiral stair to the home office, and the boot-bench and coat and bag storage corners.

PART THREE

HARMONY

BEFORE THERE'S A HOUSE, there's a piece of land. And there's always a story behind the selection of the piece of land. Some of us look for a site close to the sea or high in the mountains. Others prefer farming communities, small towns, or big cities. We'll search for a piece of property with a defining landscape feature, such as a running stream, a stand of trees, or a garden plot. Whatever the site, every piece of property has cer-

tain universal attributes. Every spot has sun or shade, seasonal breezes, and changes of light over the course of a day. Every piece of land has a view, whether it's a single tree, an uninterrupted view of the evening sky, or a romantic view of a snow-capped mountain. Every house is surrounded by countryside, neighborhoods, or a blend of the two.

If a house isn't in harmony with the land, the inherent qualities of the property will lie dormant. While any shape, any arrangement of rooms, or even any style is valid for any location, harmony is most easily achieved when the setting is respected. When a view cannot be appreciated, when natural light cannot make its way into the interior, when there is no

easy access to the outdoors, the house is not taking full advantage of its setting. Furthermore, when its exterior clashes with the landscape or the neighboring houses, then it is not in harmony with its surroundings.

When a new home is built in harmony with the setting, it looks as though it was always meant to be there. The key to creating that desired harmony is to look at the property with a fresh eye, see what it has to offer, and then choose good parts that celebrate the surrounding landscape.

CHAPTER 9 | Taking in the View

EVERYONE APPRECIATES THE VALUE OF HAVING a good view. One of the reasons my own property in upstate New York was relatively inexpensive was that it apparently had "no view." Yet once I built my house on the lot, visitors would invariably comment on the great view. How could that be? My house may not have a view of snow-capped mountains or pounding surf, but through the use of a few good house parts I was able to capture a dynamic view of the outdoors.

Good house parts can help craft a view for any property; for example, expansive walls of windows and even small "punched" windows can frame the vista. I placed my own house on a knoll that allowed me to align a window wall with a nearby hill on an adjacent property. Once the right window arrangement was in place, the simple roll of the land looked like a scene straight out of a Currier and Ives print. For another location, windows might focus the view on a hedgerow of trees or a stone wall. Properly framed with a good window arrangement, any one of these outdoor scenes would call to mind a romantic painting, which is the perfect recipe for a great view.

A home that's fortunate enough to have a view as stunning as this seaside retreat should be as transparent as possible. The wall of glass not only makes the most of the view but also expands the apparent size of the room.

Floor-to-ceiling windows are "ganged" together to form walls of glass, giving any interior a strong connection to the outdoors.

RIGHT With two walls of windows, this family room feels like a sun-room for all seasons.

CENTER This addition has a great room overlooking the country-side, with two sets of windows stacked for an impressive view.

RIGHT This small living room appears much larger when a series of floor-to-ceiling win-dows, ganged into a prow shape, expands the view of the outside and the sense of space on the inside.

GANGED WINDOWS

RIGHT The arrangement of these ganged windows mimics the layout of the backyard landscape. The tall center window frames a dominant tree, while the shorter flanking win-dows focus on flowering shrubs and grasses.

ABOVE This octagon sitting room takes advantage of its shape with windows on every wall providing a panoramic view of the sea.

Fitting windows tightly against each other where two walls meet brightens up the space and gives the illusion that the corner has dissolved. The double-hung windows open for cross ventilation and allow views into the side and backyards.

Capturing Expansive Views

The best way to capture a broad view of the landscape is to use a "gang" of windows, which is created by grouping windows tightly together, side by side, with little or no wall in between, above, or below them. There's a world of difference between a wall of windows and a picture window or a traditional bay window that is typically used to frame a view. The ganged windows create a fully transparent surface that lets you see everything from the foreground to the horizon. Even a modest landscape will seem grand when seen through a gang of windows.

When the interior is connected to nature through a stretch of windows, the home gains a sense of harmony. Small rooms feel larger by visually borrowing the expansive space of the outdoors. Large rooms seem warmer and more sen-

sual when they take advantage of the natural elements. A room with ganged windows on more than one side is particularly effective because it gives the impression that you're inside and outside at the same time.

Imagine a room with four ordinary windows on two outside walls. The unimaginative layout would

A band of casement windows frames the garden outside to create a mural-like effect on the walls of this dining room. The continuous length of sill and upper casing tie the windows together.

LEFT AND RIGHT A small fixed window is perfectly placed and sized to frame a great view, while another is festively trimmed for a view of just the sky.

The arched shape of this oversize window echoes the form of the mountain range beyond. Multiple panes match the style of the windows on the rest of the house.

This tiny window acts like the aperture on a camera. When it is open, it appears to magnify and intensify the rays of light streaming through its frame.

Placing a small punched window to either side of a bed provides glimpses of the landscape without sacrificing privacy.

RIGHT This round punched window frames a snapshot view of the side of the house and adds an architectural focal point.

LEFT When viewed from an angle, it offers an expansive view of the bay.

tection, which can be achieved by the thoughtful use of oversize windows and punched windows.

Oversize windows are single windows that have unusually large dimensions, such as 4 ft. wide by 6 ft. tall. They can be used for dramatic effect in any room. For example, a colonial home with traditional double-hung windows can incorporate a carefully placed oversize double hung for added drama and better views.

One arched-shape, oversize window can be set into a solid wall to perfectly align with a flowering tree, providing a strong connection to the landscape yet still leaving wall space for furniture or art.

Punched Windows

At the other end of the scale are small, perfectly round, oval, or square windows, which create a unique view of the landscape. They are called punched windows because they appear to be

stamped out of the wall like holes punched in decorative metal.

Punched windows offer a degree of privacy and are appropriate for walls facing a busy neighborhood street. But they add a dash of harmony to any room because they bring nature inside in unique, controlled ways. The funneled light that passes through a punched window can re-create the rays of sun passing through a partly cloudy sky. Their shape can call attention to the smallest detail of nature, such as the bark of a tree or a dense cluster of leaves. Grouped together, they can decorate the interior with tiny vignettes of nothing more than sky.

CHAPTER 10

The Nature of Materials

THE EXTERIOR MATERIALS—THE ROOFING, siding, and masonry—are the parts of a house that can best bring a home into harmony with its surroundings. Materials create harmony in two ways. First, the right choice can preserve the regional heritage of a home, for example, a renovation in a Spanish Colonial neighborhood in Florida will harmonize with the historic character of its block when the homeowners opt for tile roofs and a stucco exterior. Second, the right materials can help a home blend in with the countryside or the immediate landscape. For example, when a new house in a small Rocky Mountain town is built with heavy timbers and local stone, it reflects the rustic simplicity of the area.

The qualities of nature's resources, such as the iridescence of stone or the variegated, tree-bark-like colors of wood shake shingles, are difficult to replicate with synthetic materials.

Choose appropriate materials for your house by looking around the neighborhood to discover the prevalent materials. Then bring samples to the site to see if they go with the natural features of the landscape. Consider the texture of the materials and how they will be affected by sunlight. Smooth, shiny materials like aluminum or painted wood siding with a satin finish will reflect the sun like a bright new penny. For a house to blend into the woods, it requires materials that have a textured surface, like rough-cut wood siding or stones that will absorb the sun into their textured surfaces.

A structure looks harmonious with its landscape if it is clad in natural materials. The stacked fieldstone walls of this carport look as if they emerged out of the ground. The timber posts resemble branched trees and are stained to look like bark.

Wood siding comes in all textures and patterns.

LEFT A cladding of 8-in.-wide boards that come together with a V-shaped groove joint is painted with a satin finish to add a refined pattern and smooth texture to the gable of this waterfront cottage.

RIGHT A similar vertical siding, but without the groove, is rougher and stained a barn red to give this carport in the country a more agricultural appearance.

Wood Siding

Wood siding can be smooth as glass or as rough as the bark of a tree, and there's no limit to the color or finish that can be applied to it. Different types of wood siding look more appropriate in particular regions, depending on the wood species, the cut of the wood, and the finishes that are typically found locally. For example, a house set on the New England coast looks right at home clad in a sun-bleached cedar shingle, whereas a cottage on the moist marshes

This new house set in the rolling hills of the Hudson Valley is sided with a smooth vertical board to give a transitional character—modern but also rural. The diamond-shaped cutouts add a slightly decorative feature that seems perfect for the house's storybook location.

PIECE BY PIECE | Wood Ages Well

The emergence of vinyl and aluminum siding as preferred exterior materials has cast some doubt on the wisdom of choosing a natural material for a home's exterior. Vinyl and aluminum may not need painting as often as wood, but they will crack, pit, and dent, and they will never mellow as gracefully as wood. A good house part like wood ages well, developing a rich texture and patina with the passage of time.

of the Carolinas is more likely outfitted in a rot-resistant, painted novelty siding.

With any wood siding, the more imperfections, the deeper the shadow; and the wider the boards, the more pastoral the appearance of the home. Appropriate for rural or rustic settings, rough-cut shakes or boards are heavily textured and work well with earth-colored stains. For a less earthy but still bucolic look, even-cut shingles combine the texture

Cedar shakes offer the most texture, like the bark of a tree.

LEFT When lightly stained, the unevenness of the cuts of wood blends with the unevenness of the natural grain color.

RIGHT More solid stains can be colored to blend into the landscape: dark greens for woodlands, silver-grays for open areas near the shore.

When all of the surfaces—walls, dormers, and roofs—are clad in similar-colored cedar shingles, a house takes on a monolithic, sculptural look.

Two types of wood siding emphasize the landscape of roof shapes on this house. Smooth vertical siding covers the gable in the foreground, wood shakes clad the dormer, and a combination of the two materials encases the cupola above.

WOOD SIDING

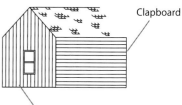

Clapboard

Board and batten

Contrasting surfaces calls attention to various parts.

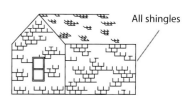

All shingles

Blending surfaces calls attention to the overall shape of the house.

Stone bricks, cut from local granite, celebrate the rough quality of materials found in this Texas region.

STONE
SIDING

These thin-cut fieldstones look like a true dry-laid stone wall but are in fact a veneer of stone only 3 in. deep. The mortar is held back, tight to the wood wall that supports the stones.

Stone can look delicate when the pieces are lighter in color and are stacked to create straight, crisp edges. The composition of the larger, quoined sandstone pieces stacked on the corner of this house, combined with the classic, graceful white painted wood details of the porch, contribute to the refined look of the façade.

look of an all-stone house. As with wood siding, one of the best ways to make a house harmonize with its surroundings is to use stones found locally. So, in the forests of New England and the Pacific Northwest, granites, bluestones, and slates are a natural choice to clad the foundations of a cedar-sided home (in the same way that they'd be found at the base of a cedar tree). Even a stone wall built from familiar stones in the landscape will help bring harmony to the home.

Blending Materials

Using more than one material on different sections of a large house is a good way to prevent the structure from overwhelming its landscape. If a house in a country village backs onto a forested area, the front might be clad in a narrow clapboard while the back façade might be dressed down a bit with even-cut shingles with a stone base.

Blending brick, stone, and stucco with wood can be a matter of complementing finishes or contrasting them. Perfect cuts of limestone will match smoothly sanded wood trim and posts that have a high-gloss finish. Rough slabs of fieldstone can pro-

Using contrasting textures of the same stone offers another opportunity for a home to harmonize with the character of its surroundings. Here, the walls are rough-cut stone, while the windows have a smooth-cut stone at the sill and in between and are capped with a chiseled stone.

Stone textures combine with wood trim on this new home to mimic the palette of the historic homes in the neighborhood.

ABOVE Heavy timber is used at the covered entryway of this stone and wood mountain lodge. Though the timber does not actually hold up the stone, it is amply proportioned to appear to do so.

LEFT The inner courtyard of this wood-shingle home features a stone wall veneered in large, boulder-like stones that are only 4 in. thick. The cut of the stone, the deep reveals between the stone, and the one large stone over the outdoor fireplace give it the beauty of a solid stone wall.

vide a transition to the roughness of the landscape at the base of a home.

Adding stone, brick, or stucco is an opportunity to harmonize a house with a region that has a variety of textures and styles in the landscape. Timber trim works well with stucco to give a smooth and rustic appearance, while brick and stone work equally well as accents. Wood and stone in all their variations from regal to rustic can be blended together for an effect that suits every nuance of the setting.

CHAPTER 11 A Place for the Outdoors

VILLAGE STREETS LINED WITH HOMES WITH open porches appear friendlier and more peaceful than those without relaxing gathering spaces. Open porches and other outdoor rooms, such as screened porches, gazebos, balconies, and widow's walks, link homeowners with the community and satisfy a universal desire to live in harmony with nature.

The definition of an outdoor room is broad, ranging from a tiny balcony off a second-floor bedroom with just enough room for a chair or two to an expansive porch that wraps around the entire first floor of a house. An outdoor room transforms a house in a number of ways. It provides an opportu-

nity to create a transition space between indoors and out. Placed strategically, an outdoor room can frame a distant view of a garden, a favorite tree, a hill, or a body of water, in much the same way that a window arrangement frames a part of the landscape.

An outdoor room also extends the living space beyond the walls of a house. Whether attached or detached, an outdoor room offers another place to hold activities or simply to sit and relax. And there's another benefit to adding an outdoor room to a house: A porch requires little maintenance other than the occasional sweep of a stone or wood floor.

The Versatile Porch

The most versatile outdoor room is the porch. It come in all shapes and sizes and is one of the most cost-effective ways to add space to a home.

It's important to choose the right location for a porch. Though a front porch improves a home's curb appeal, a porch that's placed in a private spot with better views will likely be used more frequently. Adding a porch to the outside of a rarely used din-

A double-height porch gives the homeowners the opportunity to capture views of the neighboring mountain peaks from inside and out.

Oversize pillars frame a view of the bay and create an intimate retreat under this porch.

Adding a porch to a little used area of the property—in this case, a side-yard door—can transform it into a favorite hang-out. This porch is barely 5 ft. deep, but the classical detailing of the thick columns and balcony railings above give it a grandeur and formality of a much larger structure.

ing room or spare bedroom can give those spaces new purpose and function. The rooms will be used more often as people circulate through the spaces to reach the porch. Doors that open onto the porch will also improve the amount of sunlight that streams into the room.

The classic front or side porch runs the length of one side of the house, but a porch can also protrude from a house like a wing or wrap around two or more sides. A winged porch takes full advantage of the landscape. For example, a porch with east and west exposures benefits from both morning and evening light. Winged porches can also create cozy courtyard spaces and give a square house an L- or U-shaped layout.

Wraparound porches can be designed with the same details on all sides or with different details to achieve a more varied look. If you're varying the details, preserve a sense of harmony by using only one period or style of architecture and choose from a limited palette of colors and materials.

This wraparound porch provides the house with a transitional space connecting indoors and out. The rhythmic use of columns, trim, and railings lends a soothing sense of order.

PARTS IN DETAIL Elements of a Porch

Matching the details of a porch to the architecture of the rest of the house is necessary for harmony, but the choices for materials and finishes should also work well with the surrounding landscape.

Porch posts can be simple "off-the-shelf" Doric-style columns, whose basic shape will go equally well on the banks of the Mississippi or in the woods of New Hampshire. Traditionally these posts are painted a classic white, but when painted a hunter green or barn red they take on a more rustic, camplike appearance. For even more woodland character, custom-cut timbers, stained with a clear or natural color, will blend into the surrounding trees.

Railings come in all styles. Smooth round balusters are appropriate for a delicate, ornamental railing, while flat boards used as balusters give a more casual appearance. A popular modern solution is to use metal cables and wires, which are nearly transparent, at the porch's edge.

Flooring should be made of a durable, natural material both to withstand the weather and blend with the landscape. Stones, such as slate, limestone, and granites, are great for porch flooring. Wood flooring is more affordable and can be stained or painted in any color appropriate to the home's surroundings and character.

Every detail of this simple screened porch blends perfectly into its surroundings. The stone floor matches the color of the dry earth that surrounds the house, the rough-hewn wood appears to have been gathered from the few nearby trees, and the window and door openings express the character of the local historic architecture.

The Sanctuary of a Screened Porch

A screened porch is another type of transitional room. It is furnished like an indoor room but detailed nearly the same way as an open porch—with columns, railings, and roof.

Screened porches can be designed in more creative ways than interior rooms because they're less constrained by the waterproofing and heating needs of the interior. The walls of porches are created with a variety of lacy-thin posts and beams in combination with large expanses of screening (which is much more economical than a wall of windows).

The qualities of a screened porch are quite different from those of an open porch, where nothing separates its users from the outdoors. The screens serve as a gauze curtain, softening the intensity of the natural light (and keeping the bugs out). They both expose and frame the view of the outdoors with the same drama as an expansive wall of glass but with a coziness that often escapes modern homes that are made of glass. It's the exposure to the scents, sounds, and the untempered outdoors that makes a screened porch such a magical getaway.

Opening wide the French doors and windows allows the breezes, sunlight, and scents of nature to flow freely across the porch and into the house.

ABOVE Locating a screened porch on the second floor takes advantage of upper-level breezes.

LEFT The homeowners chose stone over wood flooring so the screened porch would look more like an outdoor terrace than a more finished interior space.

LEFT At the top of this tiny beach house, a wraparound lookout is sized just deep enough to fit a couple of chairs. A thin top rail and a low trellis railing let sunlight filter through to the interior.

RIGHT Each step of the way on this wraparound covered walk gives the homeowners a different view of the ocean.

A screened porch on a second floor has a unique character. Since the space is higher off the ground, it can feel like a tree house. The circulation of air is different on a second-floor porch as well, as the breezes skimming the treetops are cooler than the air closer to the ground.

Balconies and Widow's Walks

Long ago, lookouts were familiar house parts. These were small balconies and platforms on the upper floors from which the surrounding countryside could be surveyed for news of returning loved ones and community events. Today, we rely on other means of communication for news from afar, but house parts such as balconies and widow's walks (traditionally located on a rooftop with a view of the

ocean) can still be used to bring the charm of an earlier age to a new or renovated home.

Even the smallest balcony, with just enough room to stand or to accommodate a single chair, can be a place for peaceful communion with nature. Secluded outdoor spaces provide a retreat from everyday activities, a place where you can step aside from your daily routine. Children climb trees, dangle off sills, and perhaps even venture onto a roof just for the sensation of being up high or simply to be alone for a moment or two. Adults, too, can still benefit from these away spaces. While a window can easily provide a view, a pair of French doors off a second-floor bedroom with even a sliver of a deck or a tiny threshold offers much more. These outdoor spots, perched off the side or on top of a house, satisfy the occasional need for relaxation or inspiration or just to survey the weather.

This narrow balcony curves out at one end to accommodate two rocking chairs.

RIGHT A pair of French doors gives easy access to this small 5-ft.-wide by 3-ft.-deep balcony off the master bedroom.

Balconies are intentionally placed up high on a house and left uncovered to allow for unobstructed views of sun, sky, and landscape. This tiny balcony was an added bonus when a covered porch below was built outside the side door of this bayside retreat.

CHAPTER 12 | Meeting the Land

HOMEOWNERS TYPICALLY GIVE A LOT OF thought to choosing parts like windows and doors and to adding porches to connect a home to the outdoors, but they seldom spend much time thinking about the house parts that are needed right where the house meets the ground. How well a house meets the land determines how harmonious it looks and feels. Harmony is achieved when the house and the landscape appear to be at ease with each other.

Making a house attractive at its base where it connects to the landscape is difficult to achieve because the ground is naturally uneven. In addition, houses are built on foundations that rise above the surface

A moss-covered brick terrace with granite edging is intentionally kept low to the ground so it merges with the lawn.

of the land. The exposed concrete or concrete-block foundation usually looks bare and unfinished and breaks the house's connection to the earth. But any foundation can be spruced up with the addition of a few simple good house parts that link the home with its site. For example, steps, terraces, patios, and decks can all be used to create a smooth vertical transition between indoors and out.

A set of well-designed steps at the front door will not only hide the exposed, stark foundation but will enhance the site by integrating the house with the landscape. Exteriors with prominent lines and focal points, such as carefully placed terraces, stone walls, or steps, give the entire property a sense of cohesiveness and comfort. When the edges and transitions of a home are neat and well organized, everything that leads up to them and springs from them looks purposeful.

To reduce the gap between the front door and the yard, a series of platforms fans out in several directions for an easy-to-climb link from house to land.

The broad expanse of stone steps brings this covered terrace close to the ground. The low steps eliminate the need for railings that would otherwise block the views and the sense of openness.

The stone retaining wall helps this sloped piece of land look level, creating a finished connection from house to ground.

To accomplish the simple transition from porch to land, this flagstone stoop is set flush with the grass.

The same limestone floor that runs throughout the interior, screened porch, and outdoor terrace provides visual continuity and a natural surface that meets the grass beyond.

Stoops, Steps, and Landings

To get into a house, you typically have to take a step or two up. The interior floor may be anywhere from 6 in. to 2 ft. above ground, depending on the way the house is built (wood-framed floors need to be high off the ground to prevent rot). A harmonious flow from the interior to the exterior requires a comfortable transition from raised floor to the ground below.

Stoops (platforms just outside the door), landings, and steps are vital house parts for a successful connection to the outdoors.

Large stoops, covered or uncovered, that are nearly level with the interior provide a graceful indoor/outdoor transition. Choosing the right materials for a stoop has as much to do with the landscape as it does with the style of the home. In a rural setting, for example, stoops laid with rough-cut stones blend harmoniously with the surrounding fieldstone walls, while a beach house might be better off with a glossy painted stoop to complement the brightly reflecting sand.

A set of steps can be a strong feature in its own right when it has a distinctive finish—for example, wood steps painted bright red at the entry to a Victorian cottage or a set of precisely cut granite steps in front of a formal, white-painted colonial. At a certain point, broad and deep steps become large enough to be used as an outdoor perch or as part of the entertainment space, blurring the distinction between steps, landings, and terraces.

The stone wall of this eighteenth-century farmhouse terrace joins the house to the land and creates a platform for climbing hydrangea.

Patios, Terraces, and Decks: Places in Between

Patios and terraces are the ideal link between a house and the landscape. Typically level with or just a couple of low steps down to the surrounding ground, these "in-between" places soften the experience of moving from one environment to another, such as walking from the dining room into the

ABOVE The walkout basement area rarely gets a lot of attention, but this stone terrace shows how a little planning can help blend the area with the landscape. The wall flows right into the stone landscaping and acts as a garden backdrop on the steep side of the house.

Multiple terraces along an approach to a home create a series of outdoor places that encourage visitors to pause and enjoy the garden or the surrounding views.

LEFT Thin metal railings provide protection while allowing maximum views of the woodlands from this high deck.

CENTER Combining shingle and metal railings gives this deck an open look.

RIGHT A fine metal mesh curtain offers uninterrupted—but safe—views of the water.

backyard. With their natural appearance, stone and brick patios are excellent transitional house parts. Viewed from the indoors, they provide an ideal foreground to the gardens or views beyond; from the outdoors, they can relieve the expanse of a large home or add grandeur to a more modest one.

Wood decks are an affordable alternative to stone and masonry terraces, but they must be carefully designed to make a harmonious transition between house and ground. All too often, decks are placed high off the ground and are awkwardly accessed by a single, narrow set of stairs from the yard. A smooth and natural flow can be achieved, however, by adding levels to the deck, so the platforms seem to cascade gently from house to lawn.

The way a deck meets the ground is one of the most important aspects of its design. Broad steps, the full width of the deck on one side or another, help conceal the underside and at the same time provide a graceful transition to the garden.

The color, shape, and materials of this deck mimic a boat dock, blending well with the seaside location. Because it is low to the ground, no railings are required, which allows an expansive outlook.

A 10-in.-high wood baseboard follows the curve of the screened porch wall above and conceals the concrete posts that support it.

Trimming the Base

Making the bottom of a house as attractive as the rest of the house can be challenging. Often, plantings are used to hide the foundation, but a sprinkling of greenery rarely succeeds and can be a maintenance problem.

Fortunately, a single house part can make a house seem like it's sitting on a harmonious base, rather than being suspended carelessly off the ground by its concrete foundation. A well-defined base improves the look of both the house *and* the landscape, providing a crisp line for the eye to focus on where nature ends and the house begins.

On a wood-sided house, one choice is to trim the foundation with a continuous baseboard, or water table.

A series of simple cedar lattice strips set in between the concrete piers of the foundation add texture and pattern to the bottom edge of this house.

The bases of homes with walk-out basements are particularly difficult to trim out. Here, a continuous water table caps the concrete wall of the walk-out basement (visible at left), interrupted by window bays and a turret to add interest to the low side of the house.

The flared shingle siding at the base of this house covers the foundation and creates a profile that resembles the foot of a tree trunk.

This is a board about 8 in. to 12 in. high with a small wood cap.

Brick, stucco, or stone houses that do not have an exposed concrete foundation can still benefit from a distinct band at the bottom of the house to create an attractive base. At about the same height as a water table, the walls of a masonry house can incorporate horizontal bands of complementary materials (stone with brick, for example) or bands of profiles of the same material (molded brick or stucco shapes, for example).

When the base of the house is given a distinctive and pleasing treatment, there is no need to hide the foundation. And when shrubbery or gardens are desired, the well thought out base acts as a decorative backdrop.

New brick houses look more traditional with added base details, like this molded brick cap, which recalls those used over old stone foundations.

Woodland Sophisticate

EVERY PIECE OF LAND HAS A CERTAIN CHARACTER, whether it's a compact patch of lawn in the suburbs or a sprawling forest on the far outskirts of town. This proud weekend cottage in New England makes the most of its wooded lot by preserving the dense thicket of shrubs and trees on the property. Low rooflines, deep shadows, and rustic exterior materials—in perfect harmony with the landscape— make the home practically disappear into the woods, but that's just the intention.

Architect Charles Warren let the natural character of the property direct his choice of house parts and materials for this new home. Charles pulled together an exterior of natural materials (wood and stone) with classical house parts (columns and arches) both to complement and to contrast with the rustic surroundings. The shape and texture of weathered wood shingles will age to look like tree bark, the blue-green painted wood trim is the same color as the encircling blue spruces, and a screened porch shaped like a wave emulates the movement of the water on a nearby lake.

The choice of materials and the shapes of the exterior parts both harmonize with the landscape and blend in with the community's shingle-style bungalows. A more formal colonial cottage would have seemed hemmed in by the encroaching woodlands and would have made the indigenous surroundings look weedy and unkempt.

A large arched balcony at the entrance is a dramatic house part that draws attention upward. The oversize arch emulates the mouth of a cave in the surrounding woods.

LEFT Extra-deep windows on the bottom floor of the tower appear to be set in stone. The depth is created by turning shingle siding around the corner of the window jamb and eliminating trim to accentuate the thickness of the wall.

FACING PAGE A straight wall defines a space, but this curved screened porch wall creates an optical illusion, making it difficult to tell where the inside starts and the outside begins.

The wall detailing in the dining room makes it look as though it is an extension of the covered porch beyond the floor-to-ceiling windows. High-gloss white painted siding covers portions of the walls, and the raised column next to the built-in bookshelf appears to be part of a porch post.

To achieve this contrast, all the walls and ceilings are lined with a satin-smooth wood, painted a soft shade of off-white. The clusters of large and small windows bring in strategic pools of light. Though it seems counterintuitive, the use of smaller windows on some surfaces keeps expanses of white-painted wood walls intact as a way to lighten up the interior. Too many large windows would have brought in the dark, woodsy hues from the dense forest during the day and dark shadows at night.

The naturally finished floor—a combination of oak and maple—reflects the woodland light and gives the interior a bright warm feel, almost as if it were located along the shore rather than deep in the woods. The pattern of the narrow strips of flooring, each piece a slightly different hue, adds a cheery, decorative quality to each room. If the flooring had been finished with a dark stain or were of another material, such as stone, the look would have been heavier and more formal, especially given the classical detailing of the trim work.

A Grand Stairway

The main focal point of the interior is the stairway, which is sized and crafted for a New England mansion rather than a woodland cottage. Extra wide with a gracious, sweeping design that incorporates an arched stringer, the staircase is impressive without being ostentatious. The smooth balusters and posts are simply detailed; the naturally finished oak used for the treads, landings, and hand rail creates a single coherent whole.

The staircase is set inside the watchtower that faces the lake. From the outside, the tower is a highly romantic house part, with its rounded and tapered shape, deep-set base, and wraparound windows at the top. Inside, this storybook tower is transformed into a more classical envelope for the stairway, lined with paneled wood, framed with pilasters, and incorporating a comfortable alcove at its base.

Romantic and hidden, yet classical and bright, this sophisticated woodland cottage proves that the right blend of parts can add up to a home that is harmonious with its setting and well suited to the owners' style.

The fireplace and the graceful stairway are the focal points of the first floor. The large-stone surround is the only "camp" like house part in the interior.

Placing two windows tightly together at a corner makes the wall seem to disappear. This architects' trick is a way to make the sitting area appear to be surrounded by nature.

The natural oak, white paint, open walls, and oversize scale of the stair tower help to keep the interior bright. Well-placed windows provide glimpses of the surrounding woods.

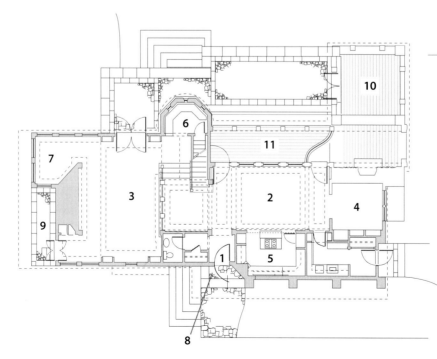

NATURE'S FLOOR PLAN

First Floor

1 Entry
2 Dining room
3 Living room
4 Family room
5 Kitchen
6 Bay-shaped alcove
7 Sitting/reading room
8 Front porch
9 Side porch
10 Screened porch
11 Back porch

Defining Part

cozy, the perfect spot to get away from it all. However, the wide doorway allows easy contact with the rest of the family's activities.

The carved-out space is filled with natural light that is reflected off the wood floor and white walls. The design mimics a great bay window overlooking the nearby lake, creating a space that embraces the local environment.

With its low ceiling, low-set windows, and big, close-to-the-floor bench, the tiny space seems especially crafted for children. But there probably isn't anyone who could resist stretching out for an afternoon nap or curling up for an early-morning read.

This alcove seems to embody the spirit of the entire house, acting as a defining accent. Its paneled walls are traditional and formal, yet the simplicity of the bench with its decorative legs is playful. The views are to the great outdoors, yet the space is protectively cozy. And the alcove's shape emphasizes privacy, yet its entryway and brightness are openly inviting.

Just as this bright, classically detailed alcove set inside a shady, picturesque tower is a freespirited combination of contrasting house parts, so is the house itself. The result proves that by building a house piece by piece—not by being a slave to a predetermined style—it can be perfectly suited to the needs of those who live within and the context of the landscape outside.

This sunny, classically detailed alcove—lined with glossy painted wood trim—is a surprising house part within the shadowy woodland cottage.

Even a relatively small space in a home, such as the area under a stairway, can be turned into a treasured corner. This alcove on the first floor of the prominent watchtower overlooking the lake has all the details that make it both comfortable and classically elegant at the same time.

Its shape is perfectly symmetrical, one half of an octagon room, and every wall surface is lined with wood trim or paneling. Deep-set windows, carved feet, and an unexpected curve soften the elegance to give the room a storybook flair. The window seat is welcoming, warm, and

QUALITY

PART FOUR

13

The All-Important Floor

The Classic Beauty of Wood Floors ✦ Stone and Ceramic Floors

14

Special Surfaces

Wainscoting ✦ Decorative Ceilings ✦ Tiled Surfaces

15

The Details That Count

Trimming Doors and Windows ✦ Ceiling Trim and Picture Rails ✦ Interior Columns

16

The Finishing Touch

Interior Doors ✦ Door Hardware

CHAPTER 13 # The All-Important Floor

FLOORING IS A CRITICAL HOUSE PART FOR shaping and delineating the interior spaces of a home. The quality of the flooring helps define the quality of the space. If it is durable, the room will be hard wearing; if it is capable of reflecting light, the room will be bright; and if it is heavily textured, the room will have a rustic touch.

The choice of flooring material influences the look of a room, the way the light bounces off the various surfaces, and the type of activities it encourages. Two rooms that have all the same house parts except for the floor can look and feel completely different from each other. A solid-wood Douglas fir floor casts a golden glow and gives a room a simple,

rural character. A stone floor can be either dark, made of large irregular pieces with rough surfaces, or brilliant, made of evenly cut pieces that are smooth as glass. A durable slate floor can make a room suitable for heavy-duty foot traffic, while a floor of knotty pine can give a room a casual ambience for recreation or everyday dining.

The Classic Beauty of Wood Floors

Most homes in the United States have wood floors. Wood floor beams hold up a subfloor layer of plywood. The plywood itself can be used as the final surface (if carefully laid and finished), but in most homes there's an additional layer for appearance's sake. Wall-to-wall carpet and sheet vinyl are generally the least expensive materials to place over plywood, but solid-wood flooring, stone, and tile are longer lasting and classically beautiful.

It's tough to match the richness and subtle variations of a solid-wood floor. Certain species and finishes bring out the individual colorations of the boards, giving the floor a pattern as bold as carpeting.

LEFT The pale yellow pine flooring reflects light off its surface and off the white painted walls to create a glow in this room throughout the day.

The wide-plank rough-cut floorboards in this room add a rustic edge to match the exposed ceiling beams and wood paneling while contrasting with the more refined limestone walls and delicate trim moldings.

LEFT AND CENTER Wood flooring in kitchens and bathrooms is softer on the feet than stone or tile and equally durable when finished with polyurethane.

RIGHT Heart pine flooring and cedar walls form durable surfaces and bring a cozy, warm character to this kitchen.

Wood flooring comes in many forms and prices, from wide-plank solid-wood flooring of exotic species to narrow strip flooring of common oak to parquet and laminated products that are sold prefinished and attach to the plywood with glue.

Solid-wood floorboards are actually slices of a tree. Floorboards typically range from 12 in. to 12 ft. in length and 2 in. to 12 in. in width. In general, the larger the slice, the higher the price. But the cost is also determined by the avail-ability of the species; thus a floor of nar-row mahogany or cherry boards may be more expen-sive than a wide-plank pine floor. Homes finished with wide-plank floors are known for their great character, but the most affordable floors are made from narrow-width oak, which is also more stable.

Two white-walled rooms with different wood floors look dra-matically different. The pale-colored pine floor (LEFT) reflects light onto the walls, lending the space a bright, contemporary feel. The dark-stained pine floor (BELOW) absorbs light and brings a warm, colo-nial character to this all-white interior.

PIECE BY PIECE | Wood for All Rooms

There isn't a room in a house that wouldn't benefit from a solid-wood floor. While more expensive than carpeting, wood is far less expensive than stone or tile, making it an ideal upgrade when redoing a bathroom or kitchen. Wood is easier on the feet than stone or tile, soft-ens the acoustics of a room, and, when protected with a good polyurethane, is easy to clean. In areas of potentially high moisture, such as under a toilet or pedestal sink, an insert of stone or tile can be added for greater durability.

This room, with dark stained wood floors, a dark wood ceiling, and brown-painted trim set against stone end walls, is a cool, cave-like retreat in a hot climate.

Solid-wood floors are remarkably hard wearing. While softer woods such as pine and Douglas fir can scratch, they can be refinished time and again by sanding them back down to a smooth finish. (Their laminated cousins can be sanded only once.) Unlike vinyl, which disintegrates over time, solid-wood floors actually get stronger, improving as they age.

As the boards lose their moisture, they become denser, harder, and more durable.

Homes with solid-wood floors seem to have brighter and fresher interiors. Wood is reflective, meaning that it bounces daylight off its surface, giving a clean, bright glow to an interior. Even dark wood floors reflect light in a way that's comparable to the effect of an expensive polished marble or granite floor. And wood can suit almost any style or character desired. For example, an even-grained

The stone floor in this attached sitting room off a bedroom makes the space feel more like a terrace. The wood floor is more appropriate for the bedroom because it is warm and soft on the feet.

wood such as cherry with a gloss finish gives a modest home a rich, refined look, whereas heavier-grained woods such as Douglas fir with a matte finish lend a country cottage look to any size home. Finally, solid wood is all natural, which means that it will harmonize with the natural surroundings of any property. Flexibility, durability, and beauty make a solid-wood floor an essential house part for every home.

Stone and Ceramic Floors

Stone is versatile—a suitable surface for any type of foot traffic and room function, and it is attractive—a material that stands out in every type of home or decor. Stone flooring comes in all sizes and thickness, so it can be easily fitted into any house. Stone is available in pure white to pure black with every shade of gray in between. Stones also come in a wide range of colors and in a variety of textures. There is an appropriate stone and stone pattern for any look, from rustic to refined. Irregular pieces of

PARTS IN DETAIL | **Using Inlay Details**

Changing flooring from room to room—say, from wood in one room to stone or carpet in another—can be a design challenge. One way to do it is to add a raised sill at the threshold between rooms, but I prefer to use an inlay detail for a more crafted, high-quality appearance.

An inlay gives a home the appearance of continuous wall-to-wall wood flooring while allowing certain rooms the added comfort of carpet or the durability of stone. For example, a carpet inlay might be used in a family room to define a sitting area for watching television, while a stone inlay would be appropriate in a foyer. With wood surrounding the areas of carpet or stone, there's no need for a raised threshold between rooms, giving the interior a more uniform, flowing appearance.

The look of inlay is accomplished by using a wood floor border that matches the flooring of the adjacent rooms. It's a simple detail for materials like thin stone and tile that are the same thickness as the surrounding wood. For thicker materials, the subfloor will need to be set lower to get a flush finish.

CHAPTER 14 | Special Surfaces

PAINT, FABRIC, AND A FEW ACCESSORIES CAN transform an ordinary room into something special, but a few good house parts can have the same—or greater—impact. And they'll last much longer and add more enduring quality to a home.

There are many options for layering good house parts onto the surface of a room. A dull, dark room that's seldom used can be turned into a space that's enjoyed every day once the walls are dressed up with painted wood wainscoting. Plain, flat ceilings can be given new life with the addition of wood beams. Colorful, shiny tiles can liven up a space that previously lacked distinction.

A simple surface treatment brings richness to a blank wall. The wide-plank walnut has a gently curved, or "rumbled," finish with a contrasting, flat piece of trim cap in the same material.

Six-foot-high wood beadboard with a deep wood cap makes this room look taller and larger than it is.

But there's no need to go overboard—not all surfaces need a distinctive accent. Special surfaces installed in just a few key areas, such as in the entryway, dining room, and kitchen, make the whole house look richer. And these permanent additions add durability and real value to a home, unlike decorative touches provided by window treatments and wall coverings.

Wainscoting

Wainscoting brings color and texture into a room. The most common application is a series of vertical strips of wood that run about halfway up a wall, but wainscoting can also be crafted from other materials, including tile and stone, and be set at any

White wainscoting on the breakfast room walls gives this space a porch-like character. Simple, wide flat casing around the windows matches the wainscoting, adding to the casual look of the room.

Even a simple light fixture looks more elegant when set against a wood bead-board wall. The contrast of metal and glass against wood emphasizes all of the materials.

WOOD WALLS

LEFT Understated wall surfaces act as a backdrop to accentuate architectural details. This horizontal Douglas fir wood plank wall serves as an unobtrusive background for the delicate carving of the stair railing.

RIGHT The slatted wood wall adds texture and a visual surprise to this interior stair hall. A smooth, solid wall would make the space feel cramped.

This contemporary cabin takes its inspiration from a log cabin and uses horizontal wood planks on all interior walls.

height. Whatever the material, wainscoting effectively brings more depth, pattern, and durability to a wall than flat decorative finishes such as wallpaper and paint.

Wood wainscoting is available in easy-to-install panels, precut to the desired height, and in traditional tongue-and-groove boards. Narrow beaded wainscoting looks great in almost any style home, but other designs can be applied to suit a specific look or style. For example, wide, rough planks, run vertically or horizontally, create the feel of a rustic cabin, while wide boards run horizontally and colored with pigmented stain give a room the character of an old colonial home. Smooth, tightly jointed wainscoting with a clear finish can bring the warmth of natural wood to a contemporary home.

When considering a painted wood wainscoting, it may be tempting to use a composite substitute instead. Composite wall paneling, made of fiberboard or fiberglass, can duplicate the pattern of elaborate wall paneling, but there are subtle yet significant differences in the quality of the finish appearance. Manufactured surfaces cannot compete with the intricate surface textures of

LEFT A wall covered in horizontal wood planking and capped with a decorative railing makes the two-story hallway look like a piece of furniture. A loft bed is tucked behind the railing.

CENTER Alderwood paneling lines the extra-deep archway leading into a stair hall, making this otherwise narrow opening seem grand.

A simple white porcelain light socket looks like a custom light fixture when set against a horizontal tongue-and-groove wood plank wall stained in a contrasting honey pine color.

natural wood, which give painted finishes their unique radiance.

While wood wainscoting typically extends no more than three-quarters of the way up a wall, walls covered entirely in wood, either with beaded boards, planking, or paneling, can have a dramatic effect on a home's interior. A room with floor-to-ceiling wood on all four walls can look stunning without any other architectural or decorative features; the wood itself creates the ambiance and serves as the main focal point.

PIECE BY PIECE | Wainscoting Cabinetry

Wainscoting can tie a room together visually. If using wood, attach the same style wainscoting and trim to walls, built-ins, and even stock kitchen cabinetry to give the room a custom integrated appearance. This lends a more architectural look to the cabinetry, allowing it to blend in with the other interior woodwork.

An arched beadboard wall adds an unusual accent in this bedroom. The partial wall divides the master suite without extending all the way up to a cathedral ceiling.

A CURE FOR ODD-SHAPED WALLS

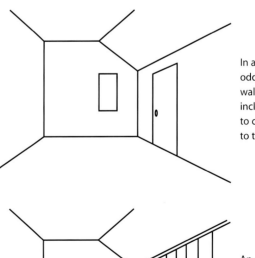

In a home with odd-shaped walls, the natural inclination is not to call attention to them.

An alternative is to sheathe the wall with wood to turn it into a special feature.

LEFT The combination of blue-painted plywood sheathing over over white, irregularly cut wooden slats creates a decorative ceiling.

RIGHT Flat trim applied to this sloped surface gives the impression that the ceiling is made of beams.

Special surfaces brighten up this cozy (but windowless) corner of a converted attic. The white-painted wood ceiling bounces light off the butterscotch-colored pine flooring and Douglas fir walls to make the room glow.

LEFT These exposed structural beams and cross ties are designed to be as attractive as they are functional.

LEFT A tapered king post slips through a set of cross ties to bring an extra layer of detail to a beamed ceiling.

RIGHT Exposed wood rafters, stained to match the planked ceiling and cross beams, give a room a rustic appearance without having to use heavier timber structures.

Decorative Ceilings

The ceiling is sometimes referred to as the fifth wall, and it's possible to use this often-neglected surface as another opportunity to improve the quality of a home.

Beams and painted wood on the ceiling can help set the character for specific areas of the house. For example, adding porchlike beams to a breakfast nook creates the feeling of eating outdoors, and colorful wood trusses or intricate patternwork can give a recreation room a playful, magical look.

It's difficult to imagine that a low-ceiling room could be improved by exposing the structural beams or adding a layer of beams. But instead of making the space seem more cramped, a beamed ceiling often makes the room feel more open, because the eye is drawn up to the patterns and architectural elements of the three-dimensional sur-

face. Another trick is to add decorative beams to the perimeter, which makes the center of the ceiling seem higher in comparison, giving an apparent lift to the room.

Although a drywall ceiling can be painted to add color to a room, a wood beadboard ceiling adds texture and pattern as well. Beaded boards, available in panels and in individual tongue-and-groove strips, are a relatively inexpensive way to construct a wood ceiling. Another option is wide, knotty pine planking for a rustic look. Smooth boards, either

A decorative wood treatment in this cathedral-ceilinged screened porch contributes a level of detailing not usually found in outdoor rooms.

ABOVE A flat drywall ceiling can be given all the drama of a cathedral ceiling when detailed with applied trim and molding.

Tiled Surfaces

Ceramic tile adds color, pattern, and durability to the walls of bathrooms, laundry rooms, and other wet areas of the home. The advent of good-quality synthetic materials means that tile is no longer an absolute requirement of a good home. Even wood can be successfully used in bathrooms and kitchens when protected with layers of polyurethane. Yet when used in combination with wood, tile can still add a spark of color and polish that makes any interior sing.

The Arts and Crafts style is famous for incorporating a few ceramic and stone tiles into furniture for an added sparkle. In the same way, glass tile in cool greens or blues used on wall surfaces in kitchens or bathrooms trimmed with natural woods will bring out the warmth of the other surfaces.

Cladding one wall in a room with white porcelain tile will intensify the natural light and brighten a dark corner. A splash of 1-in.-sq. colored mosaic tiles can bring intense vibrancy to a room without the need for added wall or window treatments.

A two-plank-wide butternut wood cap tops a wall of honed stone tile to warm up this bathroom.

RIGHT Combining ordinary tiles and wood wainscoting creates patterns that make this bathroom look much larger than it really is.

LEFT A small amount of glazed tile goes a long way. The tile backsplash accents and balances the wood cabinets and metal countertop.

RIGHT Mosaic tile can cover any shape surface, like this curved kitchen wall. The shimmering texture and earth tones of the tile complement the walnut cabinetry, room trim, and granite countertops.

TILE

LEFT This simple tile checkerboard pattern, used on only one wall of the kitchen, livens up the space while giving it the character of a summer cottage.

ABOVE Inexpensive, standard ceramic tiles come in a range of sizes and patterns. The right combination can transform an otherwise ordinary bathtub into a work of art.

CHAPTER 15

The Details That Count

OFTEN IT'S THE DETAILS THAT DETERMINE THE quality of a home. The telltale sign of a well-built home is when all the various house parts come together neatly—with no unsightly gaps or unevenness between walls and windows, walls and floors, or walls and ceiling. There are plenty of house parts that can be incorporated at these connections to ensure quality construction. Well-built and carefully placed trimwork, whether simple flat boards or elaborate built-up moldings, is an example of a seemingly small detail that can bring the entire house into an integrated whole.

This room gets its rich quality from the trimwork on the windows and walls. The 7½-in.-high baseboard and ceiling trim is wider than standard size to add substance to the space. Two wood-framed sliding doors on a barn-style pulley railing add another layer of detail.

The even divisions of the window panes and painted trim give these traditionally trimmed, double-hung windows an updated look. This same set of windows with natural finished windows and trim would have a more cottage look.

One or two special details, such as an interior column or a decorative molding along the top of a built-in cabinet, can give a modest home a sense of quality and craftsmanship. But there's no need to overdo it: Running layers of decorative molding around every surface is excessive and invariably makes a room too complicated, like too many spices in a recipe. Using decorative details sparingly, such as single-cove molding at the ceiling, brings quality to a room without gaudiness.

Trimming Doors and Windows

The investment made in good trim details can set a well-built home apart from one that has skimped on the details. Quality trimwork can make a run-of-the-mill window stand out for the same reason that sim-

Simple flat stock trim of different dimensions and in different woods and finishes creates three distinctive windows. From left to right, the trim is dark-stained walnut, painted birch, and clear-stained pine.

RIGHT A chunky baseboard, standard-width trim, and a diminutive ¾-in.-deep top cap keeps the giant 4½-ft.-wide by 9-ft.-tall window appropriately scaled for this cottage-style home.

BELOW One trim detail repeated throughout the interior can have a powerful effect. The small decorative cap at the head of the windows and doors is all that is needed to give this modern, open floor plan a more classic look.

ple, inexpensive photographs or prints look better in a good frame.

Window and door trim doesn't have to be ornate or unusual to connote quality. The simplest, most tried-and-true trim is flat stock wood casing, which, as the name implies, is a single flat board, typically ¾ in. thick. There's no one formula for figuring out the best proportions to trim out a window or door, but different widths are appropriate for different styles. For example, 3½-in.-wide trim surrounding a window results in a simple, traditional look, while a narrow trim (1½ in. by 1½ in.) provides a crisp, contemporary look.

ABOVE **The use of smooth painted trim keeps a woodsy interior from becoming too rustic. The renovation of this old colonial bungalow combines rough plaster walls, exposed wood lath, and rough-hewn beams with white flat stock trim at all windows and doors.**

LEFT **The species of wood can make a dramatic difference in the trim of a home. Douglas fir—a common wood used for porch floors and ceilings but an uncommon material for interior woodwork—is used for all the floors, wainscoting, and trim in this weekend home, bringing the character of the outdoors in.**

Solid-wood casings come in a number of species and finishes for a variety of effects. Wide knotty-pine boards with a clear matte finish say "rustic," while heavy-grained oak boards that are stained or painted in a solid color are appropriate for a Craftsman cottage. Painted wood trim with fine-grain texture, such as poplar or beech, works for any style.

Ceiling Trim and Picture Rails

A band of trim all around a room at the point where the wall meets the ceiling, or just below it, adds a layer of quality craftsmanship and a pleasing sense of proportion, even in a room with a standard 8-ft. ceiling. There are two types of trim for this purpose: crown and cove moldings, which sit flush

These three posts each have a distinct look, from the modern detail at the top of the solid mahogany piers (LEFT) to the classical capital that crowns the fluted columns (CENTER) to the branchlike brackets sprouting from a rustic interior post (RIGHT).

The entryway of this modern seaside cottage has just three details that contribute to its rich look: mahogany front doors, marble flooring, and two mahogany piers. The piers frame and enhance the matching doors and, combined with the flooring, delineate the entryway from the otherwise sparsely detailed open floor plan.

The posts in the entryway of this petite two-winged home are playfully arranged to lead the visitor to the living areas and away from the private half of the house. All the good house parts of the interior are simple and elegant, and the posts add an architectural quality.

Interior Columns

In today's homes, interior columns are usually found only in expansive, loftlike spaces, but they can add a look of quality to any interior. Whether structural or decorative, columns are sculptural elements that can be detailed to fit any architectural style. A square, tapered column with a simple flat cap and base is the hallmark of a California bungalow, while a Doric column with its classical shape, capital, and base would be ideal for a Federal town house, and a rustic timber or log column would suit an Adirondacks camp.

Columns are versatile house parts. A pair of decorative columns can set off one end of a large space from another, such as a dining area from a sitting area, without the use of walls. Using a tree trunk as a column is a unique way to bring in a touch of the outdoors, appropriate for a modest vacation retreat in the woods. The three-dimensional patternwork created by a series of custom-designed columns of solid wood combined with wood beams and brackets can make for a stunning interior.

PIECE BY PIECE | Baseboards

Solid-wood baseboards, which wrap the room at floor level, come in a wide variety of shapes, but as with other interior trim, a simple flat board is all that's needed for a high-quality appearance. A baseboard should be at least 5½ in. tall—unless it's part of the design of a modern interior with minimal trim throughout. Taller baseboards, with or without added details, provide an eye-catching custom look in a low-to-the-ground location.

One theatrical column, such as this gnarled tree post in a small bungalow, can be used as a sculptural focal point to give the interior of a home a very personal expression.

DEFINING A ROOM WITH DETAILS

A few good details transform an ordinary room into one with character and quality.

1 Picture rail unifies doors and windows.

2 Interior columns are focus of room.

3 Ceiling seems higher.

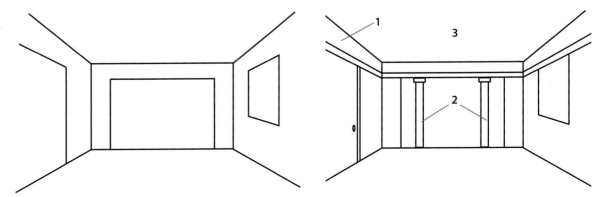

CHAPTER 16 | # The Finishing Touch

ALONG WITH WALLS, FLOORS, WINDOWS, AND a roof, doors are one of the fundamental building blocks of a home. Though homeowners take the time to shop for a quality front door, interior doors are often one of the last parts to be considered when renovating or building a new house. But when you consider the number of openings into rooms, closets, and utility spaces, it's surprising just how many doors there are even in a modest home (my own tiny, 800-sq.-ft. cottage has 12 doors).

Fortunately, interior doors don't need to be exotic or extravagant to qualify as good house parts. Every lumber-yard sells a simple, single- or two-paneled solid-wood door, which is the best door you can buy for the money. Solid-wood doors are built to last and go with all styles. They can be stained, painted, and refinished to suit any room.

The way a door works is just as important as the way it looks. Good quality door hardware—knobs, levers, hinges, and locks—can be basic yet still beautiful. There's a perfect door and matching hardware for every style and budget.

In this renovation of an eighteenth-century farmhouse, these custom-made doors capture the simple beauty of the older two-panel doors of the home. Carved finger pulls, rather than door knobs, add a contemporary touch.

Interior Doors

Interior doors should not be so ornate that they compete with other prominent house parts, such as fireplaces or picture windows. The most simple design—a flat-paneled door—is the door of choice for every residence, from a New Orleans mansion

Basic Douglas fir doors with simple black metal door knobs are used throughout the interior of this shingle-style home. The quality and beauty of a solid-wood door complements the craftsmanship of the trim, wainscoting, and continuous display shelf.

A pattern of horizontally laid panels on these doors echoes the low-slung character of this Texas ranch home. The doors are extra wide, which complements the spacious proportions of the individual rooms and hallways.

The unusual pattern of paneling on these doors reflects the unique quality throughout this house. The chunky black metal hardware, with its large face plate, gives the refined interior a touch of country informality.

to an Aspen retreat. A solid-wood paneled door is affordable and comes in a variety of species, such as pine, poplar, and Douglas fir, which can look rich with a few clear coats of polyurethane or equally impressive when painted.

One- or two-paneled doors are especially versatile. Multiple-paneled doors deliver a more specific character to a home, depending on the pattern of the panels. For example, a six-paneled door comes in two distinct versions: two panels wide and three high (which fits with colonial-style homes dating from 1750 to 1850) and one panel wide and six high (which is appropriate for homes dating from 1850 to 1950).

If you want to invest more money in a door, spend it on weight and material rather than on an ornate design. Affordable, ornate doors tend to be made of composite materials, such as a thin wood or paper veneer laminated over a particleboard base. A thicker, solid-wood door is a much better value. Every ⅛ in. of extra thickness increases the quality of a wood door. Heavier doors are often available in less common species of wood, such as walnut, alder, and mahogany, whose rich natural grain and color make them impressive without being imposing.

PIECE BY PIECE | A Uniform Look

For a consistent, high-quality look throughout the house, use the same wood species (or same treatment) for all the doors, trim, and floors. Natural pine, oak, and Douglas fir are good, affordable choices. Carry the consistency through the door and window hardware too, simply by matching their materials and finish.

Planked paneled doors add another layer of distinction to an interior. When painted, these doors work well with styles as varied as cottage casual to urban sophisticated. (Naturally finished, the doors are more suitable for a rustic or rural residence.)

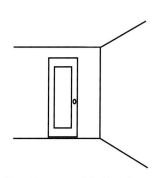

ABOVE When closed, these pocket doors add another layer of pattern to the wall. When opened, the doors disappear, allowing the room to flow directly into an adjacent space.

LEFT Inexpensive solid-wood two-paneled doors line a hallway, providing useful storage space. Tightly fitted together with a matching transom door above (to access more storage), the evenly spaced doors establish a pleasing rhythm.

DOOR HEIGHT

The height of a ceiling determines the height of a door.

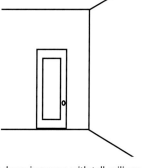

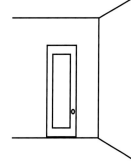

Short doors in rooms with tall ceilings look oddly proportioned.

9-ft. ceilings require 7-ft. doors.

For ceilings up to 8 ft. 6 in. tall, a standard 6-ft. 8-in. door looks fine.

Cast-metal hardware of different finishes and materials creates a look varying from rustic to elegant (from left to right, a "forged" finish on bronze, a polished stone finish on nickel, and a brushed finish on nickel).

A pair of sliding Douglas fir doors attached to a railroad track mechanism serves as a room divider. The wheel and track hardware creates a distinctive focal point, the black metal contrasting with the all-white interior.

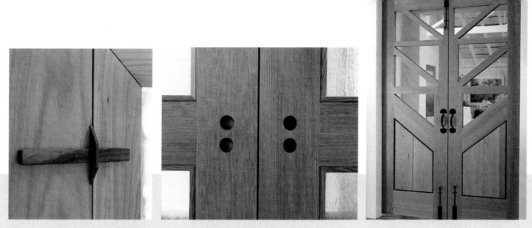

RIGHT This peg-and-slot fastener, suitable for a rustic or Asian-inspired house, holds glass or screen panels.

CENTER The craftsmanship of the routed finger pulls on these pocket doors is a sign of quality.

RIGHT Black metal pulls and antique door stays add nineteenth-century details to the updated doors.

Door Hardware

The key words for door hardware are simple, consistent, and hardworking. Though hinges go almost unnoticed, they are the most important part in terms of the way a door opens and closes. The heavier and taller the door, the more hinges are needed, though an extra hinge will make any door sturdier and easier to swing open.

To determine the quality of a hinge, simply pick it up: Better hinges weigh more. Avoid hinges that are coated with only a brass or colored finish, because they tend to show wear and tear quickly. Brushed aluminum is a good-quality, durable material that works with any style or color of door and door knob.

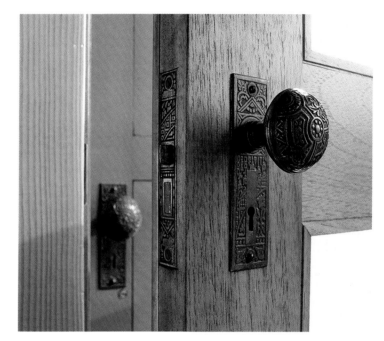

Off-the-shelf, inexpensive black metal strap hinges add a rustic, vintage character to this otherwise modern house.

Like hinges, good-quality door knobs are heavy and made of solid metal. A durable lockset (which comprises the knob, lock, and invisible internal mechanism) is more important than an ornate design. As with other door parts, the heavier the lockset the better the quality.

In terms of material for door knobs, brushed chrome works well for any clean, unfussy style, while basic black or unfinished brass is appropriate for a more traditional look. If you want a more unusual finish, knobs as elegant as jewelry or sculpture are available in nickel and bronze and in antiqued and hammered textures.

The delicate, ornate design of the antique nineteenth-century door knob and lockplate stands out against the smooth, simple, contemporary wood and glass-panel door.

Enduring the Test of Time

WHEN RENOVATING A HISTORIC HOME, IT'S all too easy to overwhelm the original bones of the house by adding on or replacing parts that don't blend in with the original parts. To preserve the quality of an older home built with natural materials crafted to withstand weather and age, the key is to select new parts that complement and enhance the old. It's what architect Peter Bohlin did so well in this nineteenth-century Rhode Island farmhouse

Elegant plank steps with a custom bent-steel railing signal to the visitor that care, quality, and a modern touch went into the home's renovation.

renovation for a family who wanted to preserve the original architecture of the home while adapting it to their modern lifestyle.

It's easy to see that this waterfront house is well built just by looking at it. The restored details, the wood shakes, and the historic style of the trim moldings used in the renovation exude a quiet grace and unassuming quality that are typical of finely crafted older homesteads. For the new parts—the raised deck, the railings, the chimneys, and the roof monitors—Peter used galvanized sheet metal, wire mesh, and steel bars. Although these materials don't seem residential in appearance, they have a humble yet enduring character that harmonizes with the rural setting.

LEFT From the classic stone wall and wood siding to the mesh rails and light monitor, high-quality traditional and modern materials blend to preserve the beauty of this historic farmhouse.

FACING PAGE The shape of the custom wood and glass door follows the shape of the roof. When it swings open, the notched door clears the bench to create a frameless extension of the hallway into the library.

Unadorned Details

Sometimes the best way to make the most of an old house's richly detailed antique parts is to frame them with new house parts that are equally well made but less grand. On this house, a set of Victorian brackets holds up the small canopy over the front door and is about the only decorative detail on the exterior renovation. More modest house parts were chosen for the other trim details; but rather than diminishing the look of the brackets, they highlight the intricacies of their design.

The house is surrounded by beautiful fieldstone walls, so it would have been appropriate to use richly detailed stone steps at the front entry door to match. But the architect purposely chose simple wood plank steps. The modest stoop blends in well with the new wraparound deck, and its modern design introduces the visitor to the surprises that await inside. The modest gesture of the front steps gives the immediate impression that the owners respect the original craftsmanship of the farmhouse while at the same time invite fresh forms of architecture so they can leave their personal mark.

COVERED IN QUALITY

First Floor

1 Stone floor
2 Slatted stair hall walls
3 Sliding barn doors
4 Custom boulder stone
5 Restored Victorian canopy
6 Wood steps
7 New stair hall wall
8 Deck
9 Wood rail
10 Metal rail
11 Den
12 Kitchen
13 Living room

(Existing house is shaded.)

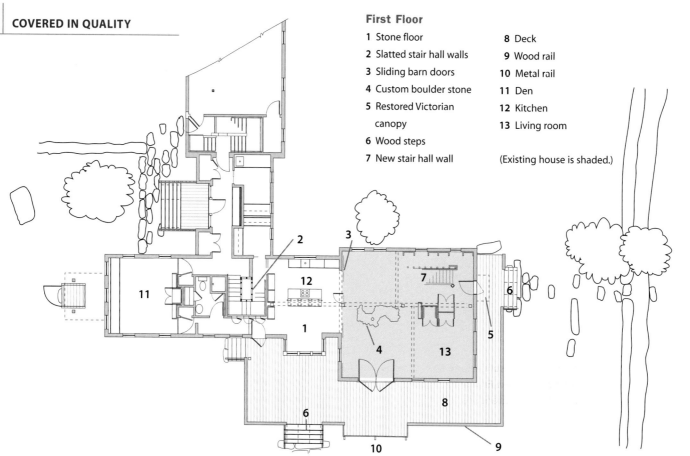

The re-sided farmhouse uses a soft palette of weathered-grey cedar shingles and grey painted clear cedar trim for a classic New England look. The meticulously restored exterior combines beautifully with the more modern interior renovation.

old-fashioned trim detail that matches the head of the windows and is finished with a lattice base that would typically be found under a wood porch. From the front, the enormous deck all but disappears from view.

On the side of the house, the simplicity of the deck's flatness and its spare detailing is the perfect foil to the grassy meadow leading down to the shoreline. Along the water side, the deck is bordered by a galvanized wire-mesh railing. This may seem like a risky way to respect the look of a historic home, but it's the architect's way of maintaining a clear view to the water. The contemporary railing also expresses something about the intended character of the home—it's the modern soul of this renovation of an otherwise traditional farmhouse.

Quality details, such as the custom open-mesh rail, the elaborate cedar knee-walls, and the cedar lattice, make this deck an appropriate addition to a historic house.

A deck was high on the owners' wish list for this waterfront home. However, a deck is not a part that fits in well with a nineteenth-century farmhouse (a wood porch or stone terrace would typically be more appropriate). A large, contemporary wooden deck might have destroyed the original charm of the house, but architect Peter Bohlin designed one that manages to blend in and maintain the integrity of the farmhouse.

The wraparound deck is ringed by an unusual guardrail that is built as a short wall clad in the same shingles as the rest of the house. It is capped with an

The light monitor and chimney are both encased in metal, giving the shingled roof added texture and visual interest. Metal boxes built around flues and chimneytops are graceful, sturdy, and age well over time. Cedar-clad gutters (right) are another quality detail that contributes to this house's enduring appeal.

A Traditional Farmhouse Roof

A cedar-shingle roof is long-lasting, weathers well, adds a layer of texture to the house, and is appropriate for a New England farmhouse. While the wood roof itself is traditional, the added details—built-in gutters, metal-clad chimneys, and light monitors—express the innovative quality of the renovation. There would be no clue that the roof has gutters at all if it weren't for the beautifully designed wood-clad leaders. The gutters are built into the edge of the roof and wrapped with wood trim to make them invisible. As a result, the house has an uncluttered roof edge, which expresses the simplicity and minimalism of the design of the renovation.

The most modern features of the exterior are the combined chimney/light monitors. Placed at strategic locations (such as above stairways), the monitors open up the roof to bring light into the interior. Though modern in design, they have their roots in the pop-up windows typically found on old farm sheds. The rhythm of finely crafted metal-clad chimneys and light monitors provides dramatic contemporary focal points that are at the same time in harmony with this house's rural roots.

Accents Old and New

The interior of the old house has been restored, remodeled, and added onto a number of times. Its most distinctive feature is the unusual staircase with a striking dual design located just inside the front

RIGHT In the restored upstairs hallway, the original staircase railing is left in place on on side and combined with a new railing on the other. Where a wall that closed off a too-narrow room (at left) once stood, a screen wall of precisely cut lumber now recalls the original farmhouse construction. New built-in storage throughout transforms the hallway into a useful library.

ABOVE Attention to detail is particularly evident in the new Douglas fir stair rail. The rounded top portion of the handrail is carefully notched at an angle to fit onto the straight-bottomed board.

ABOVE A new bedroom, lined with Douglas fir and detailed with modern built-ins, is tucked into the old attic. All of the new additions are highly contemporary in their design but have a warmth that suits the old house.

door. On one side, the architect restored the original newel post and railing to preserve a traditional look, while the other side is a modern expression of the original down-to-earth house construction.

The supporting wall that frames the stairs is not the old structure but a careful assembly of perfectly straight vertical studs supporting equally straight and evenly spaced horizontal lattice boards. The result is a modern wood wall that looks like the skeleton of the original plaster wall that once stood in its place. This type of craftsmanship, both in design and execution, is the symbol of the quality that this renovated house embodies throughout its interior and exterior.

A Minimalist Palette

The interior woodwork was renovated almost exclusively with one species of wood (Douglas fir), which gives the inside of the house its minimalist, yet warm and inviting look. The wood is of the highest "clear" quality, which means it has no apparent knots. Many

The original staircase was fitted into a front hall. With the redesign that incorporates a modern, open floor plan, the stair floats in space, revealing its sculptural qualities.

The original machine-carved newel was meticulously restored and kept as a good house part to highlight the home's history and the inventive nature of this renovation project.

of the interior details could have been crafted with less expensive knotty woods, but the clear wood is what gives the house its crisp, modern look. Using a knotty wood would have resulted in a more rustic feel, which would have clashed with the style of the original farmhouse.

Often, the simplest, plainest-looking designs are the hardest to achieve. This is true for woodwork because the more parts and details something has,

The solid, rustic quality of the massive stone fireplace is glimpsed through the clear glass panels of the extra-wide French doors. It is the only spot on the house's facade that garners immediate attention. At night, the lit fireplace is clearly the focal point of the house from inside and out.

ABOVE The new back stair of the enlarged house is more substantial and impressive than the original front stairs. While free of any ornament, the modern staircase is elaborately put together like a fine piece of furniture.

LEFT In the new wing, an eat-in kitchen is framed with a bank of double-hung windows that match the proportions of the original windows yet offer a more expansive view of the water. Fine woodwork throughout gives the interior a warm, inviting glow.

the more places there are to hide screws, nails, and other fasteners as well as awkward seams. All the new woodwork added with this renovation—the new staircase, window seat, built-ins, wainscoting, and pivoting and sliding doors—are free of any ornamental details. The individual pieces of wood come together with such tight and well-fitting joints that everything seems to be carved from one impossibly large tree. Where bolts are used, they are set in a perfect pattern, all equidistant from each other, to become a design element. And beyond that, each bolt is carefully set into a perfectly round notch, continuing the theme of quality exhibited throughout this one-of-a-kind renovation.

The bolt through this handrail is meticulously drilled into an exact-size hole so it sits clean in its setting.

Featured Architects

Please note: All photos featured in the bars are in italics.

BOHLIN CYWINSKI JACKSON
8 WEST MARKET STREET
SUITE 1200
WILKES-BARRE, PA 18701
(570) 825-8756
www.bcj.com

Rhode Island House and Guest House: pgs. 7 (right), *24 (left), 27 (right)*, 29, 30 (right), 34, *41 (center)*, 52, 71 (top left), *72 (right)*, 73 (right), 83 (right and bottom), 84 (left), *141 (center and right)*, 142 (bottom), *166 (right)*, 168, *169 (left)*, 174, 182 (right), 188, *189 (center* and right), 190-199

Waverly House: pgs. 13, *23 (right), 34 (left), 41 (right)*, 66-67, 78 (right), 111, *116*, 134 (left), *138 (right)*, 170, 177 (right), 185

Condon Residence: pgs. 5, 7 (left), 18, 25 (left), 38, *43 (left), 64 (right)*, 68, 75 (bottom), 78 (left), 80 (left), *96 (right)*, 97 (bottom right), 127, 129 (bottom), 138, *139 (center), 159 (right)*, 166, *167 (left and right)*, 181, 186 (right)

CENTERBROOK ARCHITECTS AND PLANNERS
67 MAIN STREET
POST OFFICE BOX 955
CENTERBROOK, CT 06409-0955
(860) 767-0175
www.centerbrook.com

House in the Hudson Valley: pgs. 23, 25 (right), 42, 51 (right), *64 (center), 78 (right)*, 95, *97 (right), 108 (right)*, 112 (center), 113 (left and center), 120, 136 (top), 137, 140 (top right and left), *166 (center), 180 (right)*

House in the Country, Lyme, CT: pgs. 6, 20, (left), 26 (right), 31, 33, 53 (top), *69 (left and second from left)*, 73 (right), *97 (center), 108 (center)*, 170, 179

House in the Connecticut Hills: pgs. 8 (top), 10 (right), 16, 27 (bottom), 53 (bottom), 74 (top), 83 (top), 86, 159 (top), 180 (bottom)

House in Killingworth, CT: pgs. 10 (left), *18 (left), 27 (center), 46, 53 (center)*, 75 (top), 90 (right), 91, 92, *117 (left)*, 118 (left), *120 (right)*, 154, *168 (left), 189 (left and right)*, 189 (left)

Crowell Studio, NY: pgs. *23 (left), 39 (left* and bottom), 47, 51 (left), *96 (left)*, 112 (left), 132

MICHAEL G. IMBER, ARCHITECT
111 WEST EL PRADO
SAN ANTONIO, TX 78212
(210) 824-7703
www.michaelgimber.com

Texas House: pgs. 79, *80 (left)*, 81 (left), 93 (left), 124, 129 (top), 172, 184 (left), 187 (left),

Brown Residence: pgs. 20 (right), *26 (left)*, 31 (right), *32 (left* and in sidebar), *35 (right)*, 42 (top), 44 (left), *80 (right)*, 81 (right), *86 (left)*, 113, 116, 131 (center), 139 (right), *154 (right)*, 158, 159 (bottom), 161 (left), 162 (right), 163, 164 (left), *173 (left)*, 178

Butcher Residence: pgs. 19, *38 (right), 48 (right* and bottom), *95 (right)*, 123 (right), 130, 131 (top and bottom)

Jennett Residence: pgs. 12 (left), *18 (center), 24 (right)*, 89 (left), 90 (left), *108 (left)*, 109, *124 (left), 141 (left)*, 160, *169 (right)*

Richter Residence: pgs. 22 (right), 40, 50, 54-61, 71 (right), 76-77, *78 (left)*, 82 (right), *92 (left), 117 (right), 125, 139 (right), 154 (left)*, 176 (bottom), 187 (right)

CHARLES WARREN, ARCHITECT
52 WEST 27ᵀᴴ STREET
NEW YORK, NY 10001
(212) 689-0907
www.charleswarren.com

Levine Residence: pgs. 4, *18 (right), 41 (left)*, 49 (left), 65, *69 (right and second from right)*, *79 (right)*, 88 (right), *92 (right), 94 (right)*, *96 (center)*, 108, 118 (right), *121 (center)*, 125 (left), 135, 155, 164 (top right), 173 (right), 182 (left)

Glen Arbor House: pgs. *25 (center), 40 (left)*, *44, 45, 49, 69, 72 (left), 73 (right)*, 84 (right), 87 (bottom), 97 (top), 110, *112 (right)*, 114 (right), 115, *121 (right)*, 132 (left), 156 (left), 167, 176 (top), *178*

New Hampshire House: pgs. *31 (left)*, 35, *48 (left)*, 64, 71 (bottom left), 72, 82 (left), *94 (left)*, 97 (bottom left), *112 (left)*, 143 (right), 144-151, 169, 172 (right), 183, *185 (right* and bottom right)

Seaside House: pgs. 3 (left and third from left), 21, 28, 30 (left), *34 (right), 38 (left)*, 44 (right), 50-51, 87 (top), *88 (right* and bottom left), 89 (right), *93 (left* and bottom right), 132 (right), 141, 142 (top), 152, 173 (left), *180 (center)*, 186 (left)

DENNIS WEDLICK, ARCHITECT
85 WORTH STREET
NEW YORK, NY 10013
(212) 625-9222
www.dennis-wedlick.com

Pomona House: pgs. 2, 11, *40 (right), 43 (right), 53 (left), 96 (left)*, 106, *124 (right), 159 (left)*, 165, *166 (left), 169 (center)*, 171, 177 (left), *179 (left)*

Kinderhook House: pgs. 14-15, *79 (left)*, 134 (right), 143 (top), *159 (center), 179 (right)*

Hillsdale House: pgs. 12 (right), *25 (left), 43 (center)*, 88 (left), *93 (right), 95 (center)*, 113 (right), *121 (left), 139 (left)*, 140 (bottom right), 175, *176 (right)*

Fichman Residence: pgs. 26 (left), *39 (top)*, 62, 70, 74 (bottom), 85, 98-105, 156 (right), 157, 184 (right)

Virginia House: pgs. 8 (bottom), *15 (right)*, 27 (top), *32 (right), 49 (right), 53 (right)*, 68, *73 (left)*, 81, *95 (left)*, 122, 123 (left and center), 136 (bottom left and right), 139 (left), 143 (bottom), 161 (bottom), 164 (top left), *173 (right), 176 (left and center)*, 188 (left)

New York House: pgs. 3 (second from left and right), 9, *26 (right), 27 (left), 35 (left)*, 36-37, *39 (right), 43, 64 (left)*, 74 (center), 80 (right), *86 (right)*, 94, 96 (right), *97 (left)*, 112 (right), 114 (left), 117, *120 (left)*, 121, 126 (right), 128, 133, *138 (left)*, 161 (right), *168 (right)*, 172 (left), *180 (left* and top), *185 (left)*, 187, 188 *(center* and right)

Colorado House: pgs. 22 (left), 24, 41, 42 (bottom), 119, 125 (right), 126 (left), *154 (center)*, 162 (left), *167 (center)*